MY BODY

EXPLAINED AND ILLUSTRATED

LITTLE
GESTALTEN

Sturdy Scaffolding:
THE SKELETON

If we were like jellyfish and spent our days drifting through the ocean, we wouldn't need a skeleton. But without our bones, we wouldn't be able to do things like run, jump, ride a bike, or read books. A skeleton looks kind of creepy, but we need it so that we can walk upright. It also helps look after our organs. Our ribcage protects our heart, lungs, and liver, while our skull keeps our brain safe and sound. As we grow up, many of our bones grow together. Adults have a little over 200 bones in their bodies. They're all different shapes and sizes: we've got big ones, small ones, flat ones, round ones, square ones, and tubular ones. Bones make up about 12 percent of a woman's bodyweight and about 15 percent of a man's. So, if a man weighs 200 pounds, his skeleton will weigh roughly 30 pounds. The thigh bone is the heaviest bone in the body because it's the one that has to carry the most weight. The smallest bones are found inside our ear and measure just a fraction of an inch. Oh, and did you know that giraffes have the same number of neck bones (seven) as we do? Theirs are just much longer than ours.

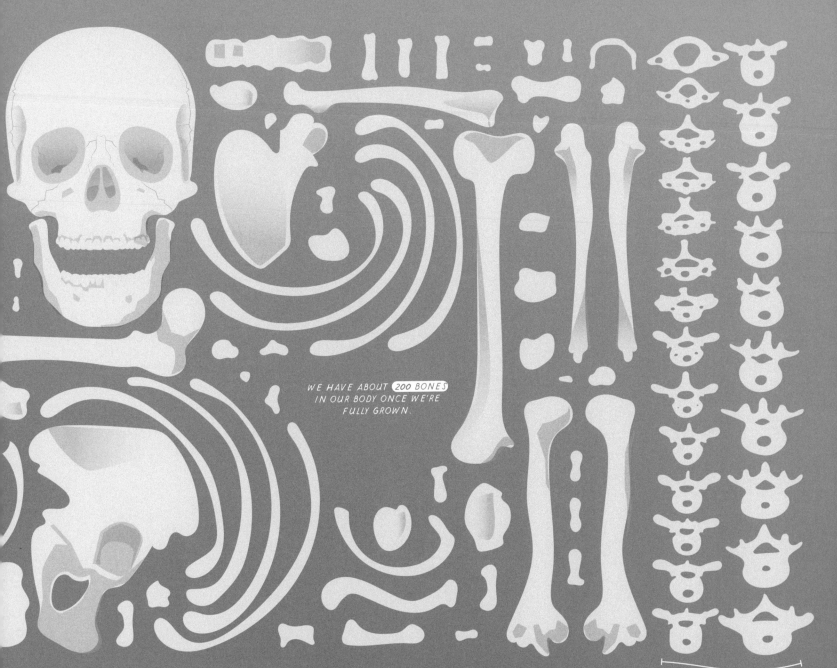

WE HAVE ABOUT 200 BONES IN OUR BODY ONCE WE'RE FULLY GROWN.

Bendy and Protective: The Spine

Our spine connects our upper body (ribcage, arms, and head) with our lower body (pelvis and legs). It is made up of 24 vertebrae and two other bones called the sacrum and the coccyx. As long as your spine is healthy and its muscles get plenty of exercise, it will be strong and flexible, and you will be able to move your upper body in almost any direction you want. The spine also protects our spinal cord. This is a thick bundle of nerves that is connected to our brain and branches off to reach all different parts of our body. Spinal discs are layers of springy material that sit in between the vertebrae and act as shock absorbers. When we go to sleep at night, the discs renew themselves by absorbing water to replace what they lost during the day. That's why adults can be almost an inch taller in the morning than they are at night!

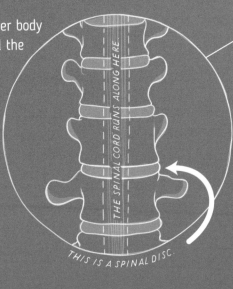

THE SPINAL CORD RUNS ALONG HERE

THIS IS A SPINAL DISC.

THESE BONES ARE CALLED VERTEBRAE. THEY MAKE UP OUR SPINAL COLUMN. THE SPINAL COLUMN CONTAINS THE SPINAL CORD, WHICH IS A THICK BUNDLE OF NERVES THAT LEADS TO THE BRAIN. SPINAL DISCS ARE LITTLE SPRINGY CUSHIONS THAT MAKE SURE THE VERTEBRAE IN OUR SPINE CAN MOVE.

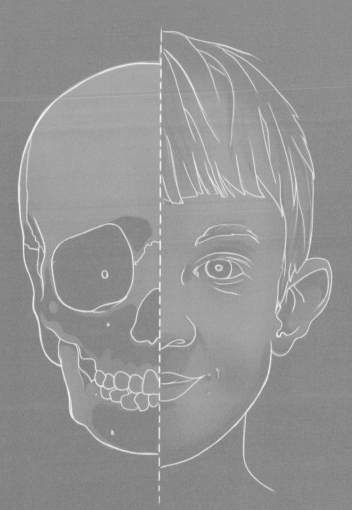

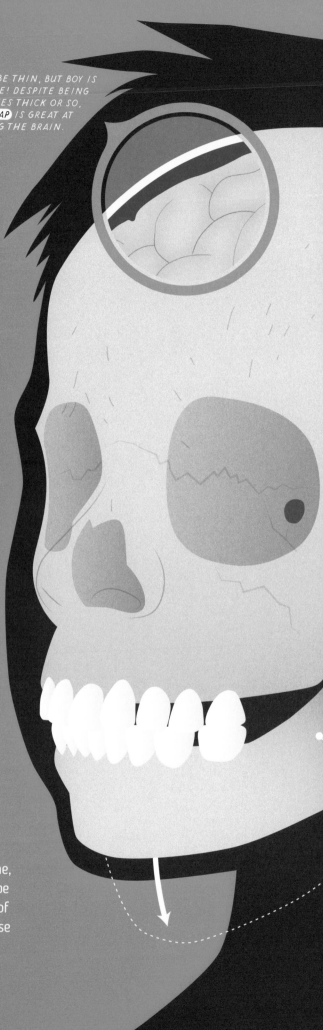

IT MIGHT BE THIN, BUT BOY IS IT EFFECTIVE! DESPITE BEING JUST **0.2** INCHES THICK OR SO, THE (SKULLCAP) IS GREAT AT PROTECTING THE BRAIN.

OUR SKULL HAS OPENINGS FOR OUR EYES, EARS, NOSE, AND MOUTH. THIS IS GOOD NEWS FOR US, BECAUSE WITHOUT OUR SENSORY ORGANS, OUR BRAINS WOULD HAVE NO INFORMATION TO PROCESS!

Natural Hard Hat:

THE SKULL

Our head contains so many important things. Our eyes, nose, mouth, ears, and brain are all neatly arranged in there and held in place by 29 bones that make up our skull. The skull is a natural hard hat. It protects our brain by cushioning our head whenever we bump it. But although it's good at its job, smart cookies will wear an extra helmet when skiing or cycling. And they'll definitely wear one if they get in a boxing ring, where powerful punches can do serious damage. Although the top of our skull might look like one big, round bone, it's actually made up of eight different sections. To make it easier for babies to be born, their skulls are soft and even have gaps in them. This allows the sections of the skull to be pressed together during birth. The gaps (known as (fontanels)) close with bone when a child is about two years old.

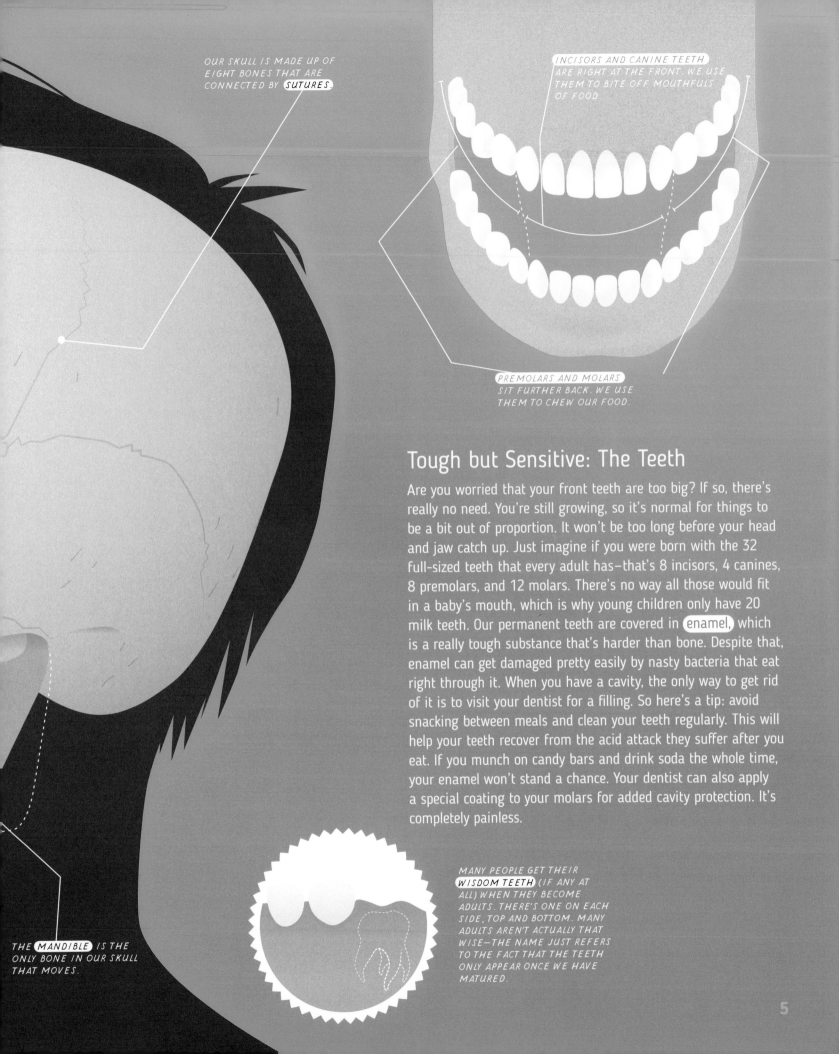

OUR SKULL IS MADE UP OF EIGHT BONES THAT ARE CONNECTED BY SUTURES.

INCISORS AND CANINE TEETH ARE RIGHT AT THE FRONT. WE USE THEM TO BITE OFF MOUTHFULS OF FOOD.

PREMOLARS AND MOLARS SIT FURTHER BACK. WE USE THEM TO CHEW OUR FOOD.

Tough but Sensitive: The Teeth

Are you worried that your front teeth are too big? If so, there's really no need. You're still growing, so it's normal for things to be a bit out of proportion. It won't be too long before your head and jaw catch up. Just imagine if you were born with the 32 full-sized teeth that every adult has—that's 8 incisors, 4 canines, 8 premolars, and 12 molars. There's no way all those would fit in a baby's mouth, which is why young children only have 20 milk teeth. Our permanent teeth are covered in enamel, which is a really tough substance that's harder than bone. Despite that, enamel can get damaged pretty easily by nasty bacteria that eat right through it. When you have a cavity, the only way to get rid of it is to visit your dentist for a filling. So here's a tip: avoid snacking between meals and clean your teeth regularly. This will help your teeth recover from the acid attack they suffer after you eat. If you munch on candy bars and drink soda the whole time, your enamel won't stand a chance. Your dentist can also apply a special coating to your molars for added cavity protection. It's completely painless.

MANY PEOPLE GET THEIR WISDOM TEETH (IF ANY AT ALL) WHEN THEY BECOME ADULTS. THERE'S ONE ON EACH SIDE, TOP AND BOTTOM. MANY ADULTS AREN'T ACTUALLY THAT WISE—THE NAME JUST REFERS TO THE FACT THAT THE TEETH ONLY APPEAR ONCE WE HAVE MATURED.

THE MANDIBLE IS THE ONLY BONE IN OUR SKULL THAT MOVES.

LOADS AND LOADS OF THIN BLOOD VESSELS RUN THROUGH OUR BONES AND SUPPLY THEM WITH NUTRIENTS AND OXYGEN.

TO STOP OUR BONES BANGING TOGETHER IN A JOINT, THEY HAVE A LAYER OF CARTILAGE BETWEEN THEM. CARTILAGE IS SMOOTH AND FLEXIBLE, AND ACTS AS A SHOCK ABSORBER FOR BONES. SYNOVIAL FLUID KEEPS THE CARTILAGE WELL LUBRICATED.

BONES ALSO CONTAIN NERVE PATHWAYS, WHICH IS WHY IT HURTS IF YOU BREAK ONE!

THE BLOOD THAT OUR BODY NEEDS IS MADE INSIDE FLAT BONES (LIKE OUR SHOULDER BLADES).

Lightweight and Strong:
THE BONES

Do you play sports? How about drinking milk? And are you a fan of cheese sandwiches? If so, well done! Cheese and milk contain lots of calcium (so do brown bread, spinach, and broccoli), which is a mineral that keeps our bones healthy. Vitamin D, which our bodies produce when we're out in the sun, is also good for bones. The more we move, the stronger our bones become. This is why athletes have heavier, harder bones than couch potatoes do. Nerves and blood vessels run through our bones, which means they're as alive as we are. The only dead bones are the ones you see in museums. Flat bones contain bone marrow, which makes our blood cells. The bone tissue that surrounds marrow is made of tiny rods of bone with lots of gaps in between. This keeps everything as light as possible—if our bones were solid, we wouldn't be able to carry our own weight!

Healing the Hurt: Broken Bones

Breaking a bone isn't fun, but it's not the end of the world. The worst thing is probably the cast you have to wear for weeks or months afterwards. The only way a broken bone can heal is if it's kept really still and fixed firmly in place. A cast is usually all you need for a straightforward break (known as a fracture). But if there are complications, your doctor will reach for the tool kit and use screws or small metal plates to hold the bones together. Once you've been fixed up at the hospital, your body starts working overtime. New bone cells appear and build new bone tissue. After a while, the break disappears and the bone has healed. The site of the fracture often ends up harder than it was before.

1 WITHIN A FEW HOURS, A BLOOD CLOT FORMS AND FILLS THE FRACTURE SITE.

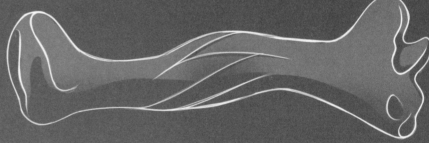

2 AFTER TWO WEEKS, THE CLOT HAS BEEN REPLACED BY SPONGY BONE TISSUE.

THE STIRRUP IS THE SMALLEST BONE IN THE HUMAN BODY. IT'S ROUGHLY THE SIZE OF A GRAIN OF RICE AND SITS INSIDE THE EAR.

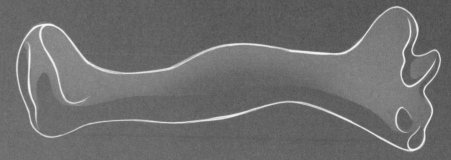

3 AFTER THREE MONTHS, COMPACT BONE TISSUE HAS FORMED AND THE BREAK HAS HEALED.

A Big, Expandable Bone:

THE PELVIS

The pelvis is shaped like a ring. It connects our legs to our body and allows us to walk. Women's pelvises are wider than men's—and they can expand! This is to help in childbirth, when the baby has to move through the woman's pelvis. A pelvis is also a bit like a bowl that holds our intestines in place. Plus, you can sit on it!

Smooth Operators: The Joints

Whenever you do a forward roll or curl up in bed like a cat snoozing in its basket, you're using your joints. If we didn't have joints, we'd be as unbendable as a broom handle. There are lots of joints in a human body. You find them wherever two bones meet. The two bones in a joint are connected by ligaments, which stop the joint from doing anything it shouldn't—like bending too far in one direction. People who have very flexible ligaments, perhaps because they stretch a lot every day, will be able to do the splits. They might even enjoy successful careers as contortionists.

JOINT CAPSULES ARE VERY WELL LUBRICATED SO THAT THE BONES IN THE JOINT CAN MOVE QUIETLY AND SMOOTHLY.

JOINT CAPSULES SURROUND BONES THAT COME TOGETHER IN A JOINT. THE CAPSULES ARE SURROUNDED BY THE LIGAMENTS THAT HOLD THE JOINT TOGETHER.

WITHOUT JOINTS, WE WOULDN'T EVEN BE ABLE TO MOVE LIKE A ROBOT. WE HAVE LOTS OF JOINTS IN OUR HANDS, WHICH ARE FULL OF LITTLE BONES JUST WAITING TO BE MOVED.

Motion Machines:
THE MUSCLES

We're packed with muscles. Whether you're a lanky kid or a muscly athlete, we all have more than 650 muscles in our body. Muscles make up about a third of a woman's bodyweight and nearly half of a man's so they're much heavier than our bones. If you do a lot of sports, your muscles will get bigger and heavier. But sports make us fitter, not fatter. The human body has three different types of muscle. Skeletal muscle is the type that we have most of. These muscles are striated (made up of crisscrossing fibers) and we can move them voluntarily. The second type is smooth muscle. It's found in organs like the stomach, intestines, and esophagus, where it helps move food through our digestive system. Smooth muscle works independently and we don't notice it happening. The third type is cardiac muscle, which makes up our heart and automatically beats as fast and as hard as it needs to.

Great Team Players:
Muscle Pairs

Most of our muscles wouldn't be much use on their own. They work best in a team of two. We've each got 320 muscle pairs. The pair in our upper arm are called the biceps and the triceps. They let us lift our lower arm. To do that, the muscle fibers of the biceps scrunch up and get shorter, while the triceps relaxes and gets longer. Try it for yourself. Bend your arm at the elbow so your lower arm points upwards, and you'll see your biceps start to bulge. Tennis and gymnastics are good for building up arm muscles. The biggest muscle in your body is in your rear and the strongest—the masseter—is in your mouth. The masseter is incredibly powerful so, if you grind your teeth in your sleep, your dentist might give you a guard to stop them from getting damaged.

THE BICEPS AND TRICEPS MOVE OUR LOWER ARM. WHEN WE WANT TO LIFT IT, THE BICEPS CONTRACTS AND PULLS THE LOWER ARM BONE TOWARDS IT AND THE TRICEPS RELAXES. TO STRETCH IT BACK OUT, THE TRICEPS CONTRACTS AND THE BICEPS RELAXES.

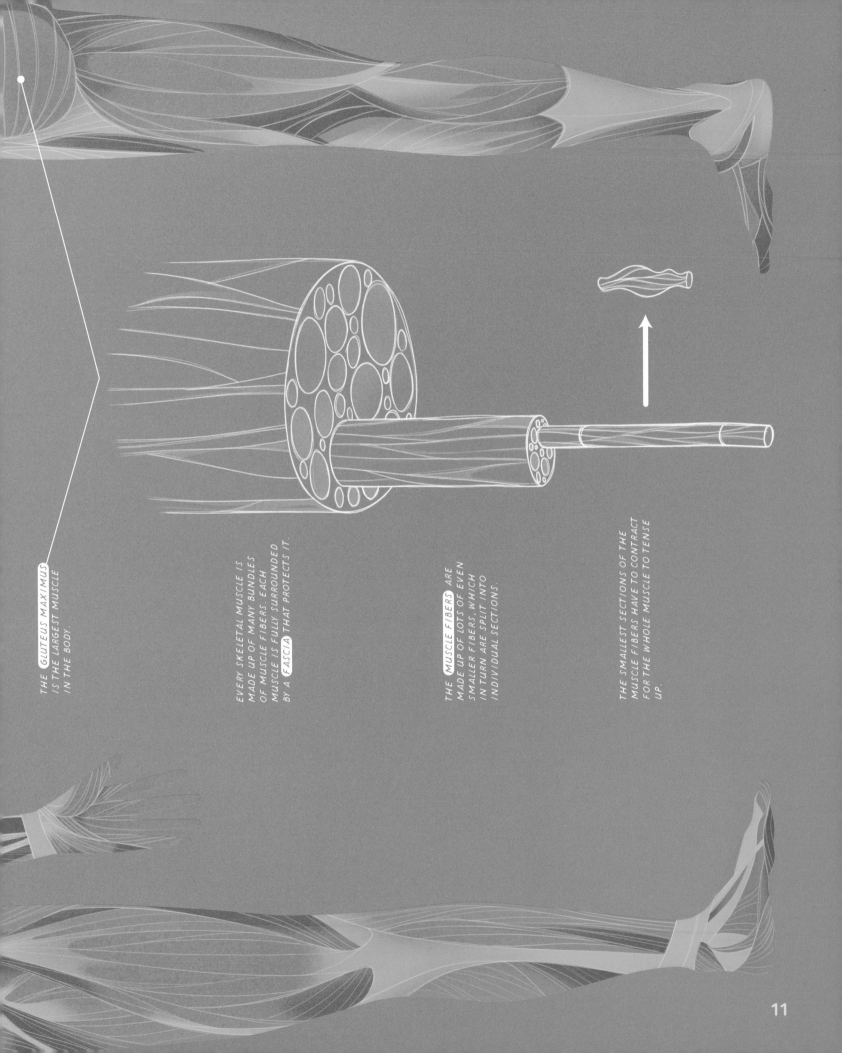

THE GLUTEUS MAXIMUS
IS THE LARGEST MUSCLE
IN THE BODY.

EVERY SKELETAL MUSCLE IS
MADE UP OF MANY BUNDLES
OF MUSCLE FIBERS. EACH
MUSCLE IS FULLY SURROUNDED
BY A FASCIA THAT PROTECTS IT.

THE MUSCLE FIBERS ARE
MADE UP OF LOTS OF EVEN
SMALLER FIBERS, WHICH
IN TURN ARE SPLIT INTO
INDIVIDUAL SECTIONS.

THE SMALLEST SECTIONS OF THE
MUSCLE FIBERS HAVE TO CONTRACT
FOR THE WHOLE MUSCLE TO TENSE
UP.

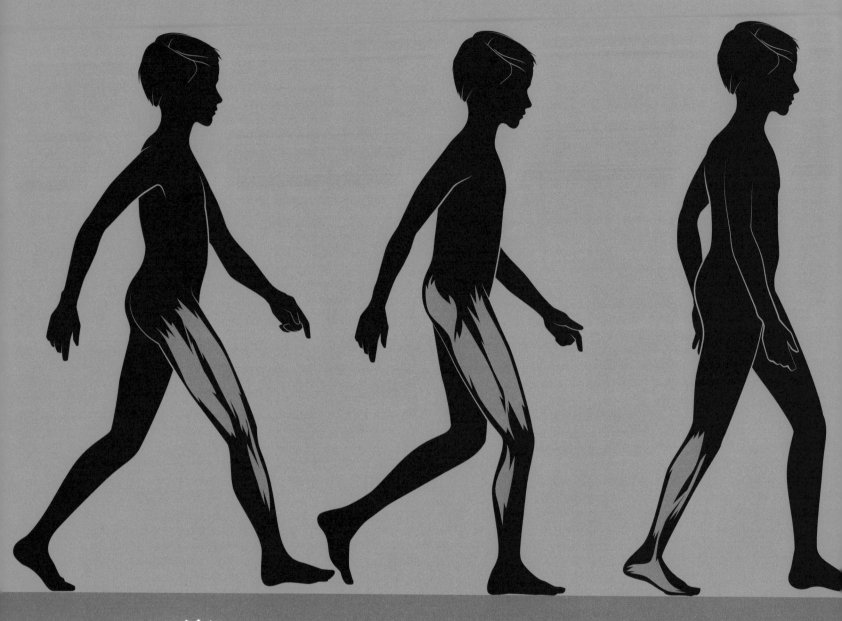

1 WHEN YOU TAKE A NORMAL STEP FORWARD, YOUR RIGHT LEG CARRIES YOUR WEIGHT.

2 IT SUPPORTS YOUR BODY AND MOVES YOU FORWARD.

3 NOW YOU'RE STANDING ON YOUR RIGHT LEG, WHICH STABILIZES YOUR BODY.

A SIMPLE SHRUG OF THE SHOULDERS MOVES EVERY BONE FROM YOUR COLLARBONE TO THE BONES IN YOUR FINGERS. THAT'S OVER 60 BONES!

Smooth and Steady:

HOW WE MOVE

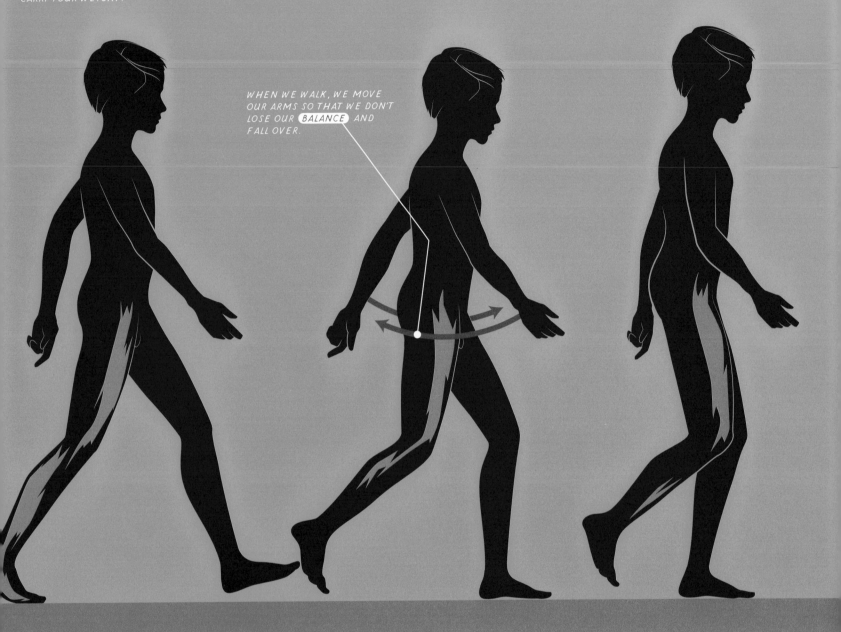

4 YOUR RIGHT LEG PUSHES YOUR BODY FORWARD, AND YOUR LEFT LEG HAS TO CARRY YOUR WEIGHT.

5 AS YOU MOVE FORWARD, YOUR LEFT LEG STABILIZES YOUR BODY.

6 THEN IT CARRIES YOUR WEIGHT.

WHEN WE WALK, WE MOVE OUR ARMS SO THAT WE DON'T LOSE OUR BALANCE AND FALL OVER.

Robots can mow lawns, play soccer, and even paint cars. But although the technology is amazing, robot movements are jerky and anything but elegant. That's because they don't have any muscles, and muscles are what allow us humans to move as smoothly as we do. Whether we're running, dancing, doing backflips, or just cleaning up our room, we always look better than a robot trying to do the same things. A single movement often requires our brain to send different signals to lots of different muscles. Most of our muscles are attached to the bones of our skeleton by tendons. When a muscle tenses, it pulls on the tendon and the tendon moves the bone—a bit like a marionette! All our muscle pairs (like the biceps and triceps) work together as opposites. If one of them scrunches up, the other stretches out and vice versa. This is the only way that a muscle can relax after tensing. If you don't usually exercise much and then suddenly do a lot, you'll probably end up with sore, stiff muscles.

13

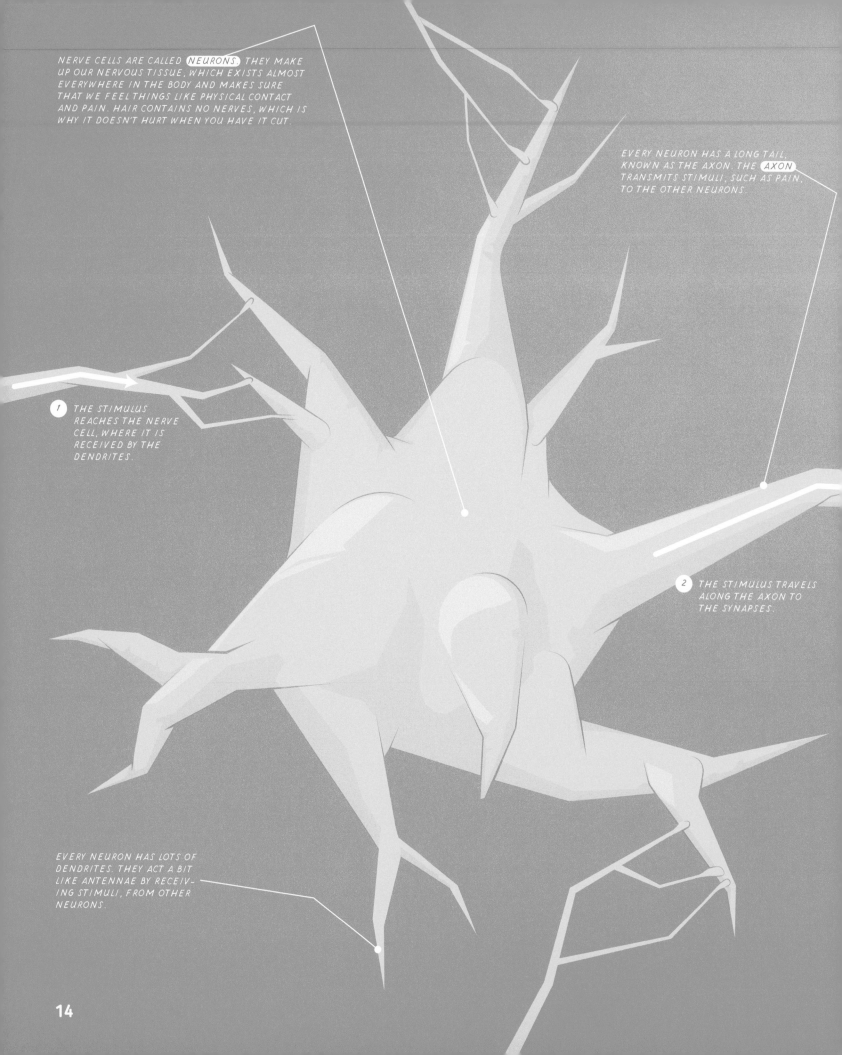

NERVE CELLS ARE CALLED (NEURONS.) THEY MAKE
UP OUR NERVOUS TISSUE, WHICH EXISTS ALMOST
EVERYWHERE IN THE BODY AND MAKES SURE
THAT WE FEEL THINGS LIKE PHYSICAL CONTACT
AND PAIN. HAIR CONTAINS NO NERVES, WHICH IS
WHY IT DOESN'T HURT WHEN YOU HAVE IT CUT.

EVERY NEURON HAS A LONG TAIL,
KNOWN AS THE AXON. THE (AXON)
TRANSMITS STIMULI, SUCH AS PAIN,
TO THE OTHER NEURONS.

1 THE STIMULUS
REACHES THE NERVE
CELL, WHERE IT IS
RECEIVED BY THE
DENDRITES.

2 THE STIMULUS TRAVELS
ALONG THE AXON TO
THE SYNAPSES.

EVERY NEURON HAS LOTS OF
DENDRITES. THEY ACT A BIT
LIKE ANTENNAE BY RECEIV-
ING STIMULI, FROM OTHER
NEURONS.

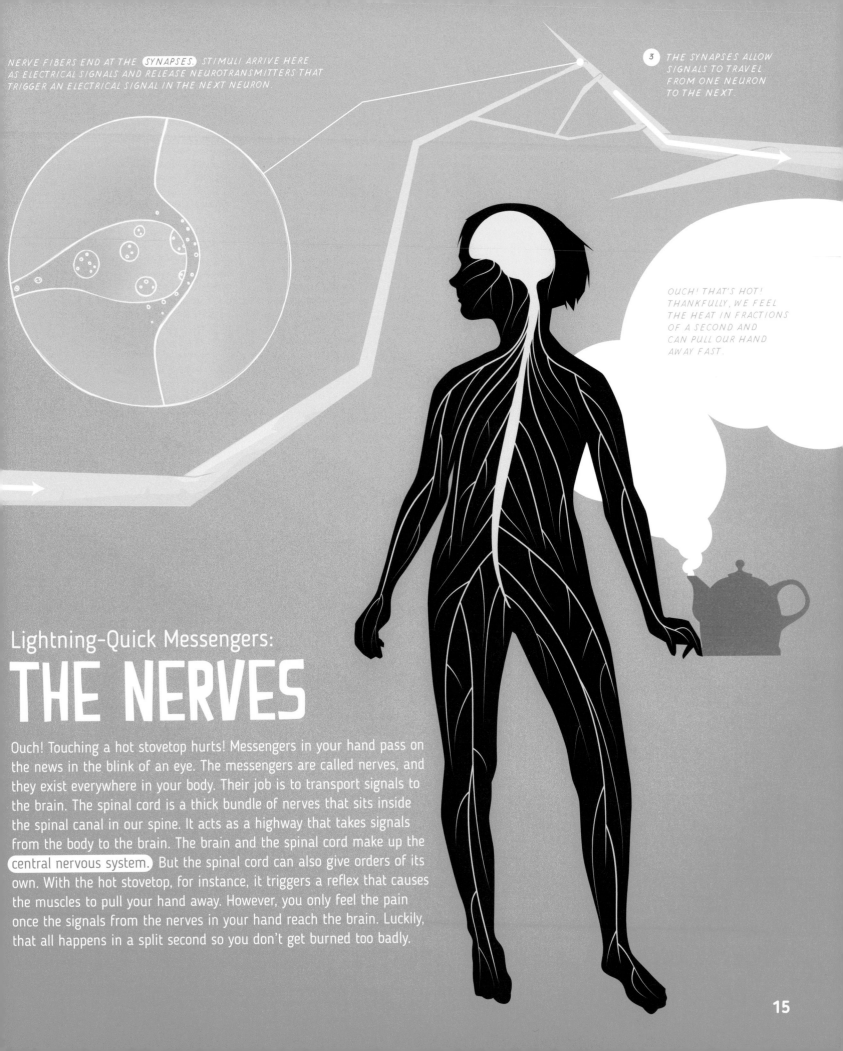

NERVE FIBERS END AT THE *SYNAPSES*. STIMULI ARRIVE HERE AS ELECTRICAL SIGNALS AND RELEASE NEUROTRANSMITTERS THAT TRIGGER AN ELECTRICAL SIGNAL IN THE NEXT NEURON.

3 THE SYNAPSES ALLOW SIGNALS TO TRAVEL FROM ONE NEURON TO THE NEXT.

OUCH! THAT'S HOT! THANKFULLY, WE FEEL THE HEAT IN FRACTIONS OF A SECOND AND CAN PULL OUR HAND AWAY FAST.

Lightning-Quick Messengers:
THE NERVES

Ouch! Touching a hot stovetop hurts! Messengers in your hand pass on the news in the blink of an eye. The messengers are called nerves, and they exist everywhere in your body. Their job is to transport signals to the brain. The spinal cord is a thick bundle of nerves that sits inside the spinal canal in our spine. It acts as a highway that takes signals from the body to the brain. The brain and the spinal cord make up the central nervous system. But the spinal cord can also give orders of its own. With the hot stovetop, for instance, it triggers a reflex that causes the muscles to pull your hand away. However, you only feel the pain once the signals from the nerves in your hand reach the brain. Luckily, that all happens in a split second so you don't get burned too badly.

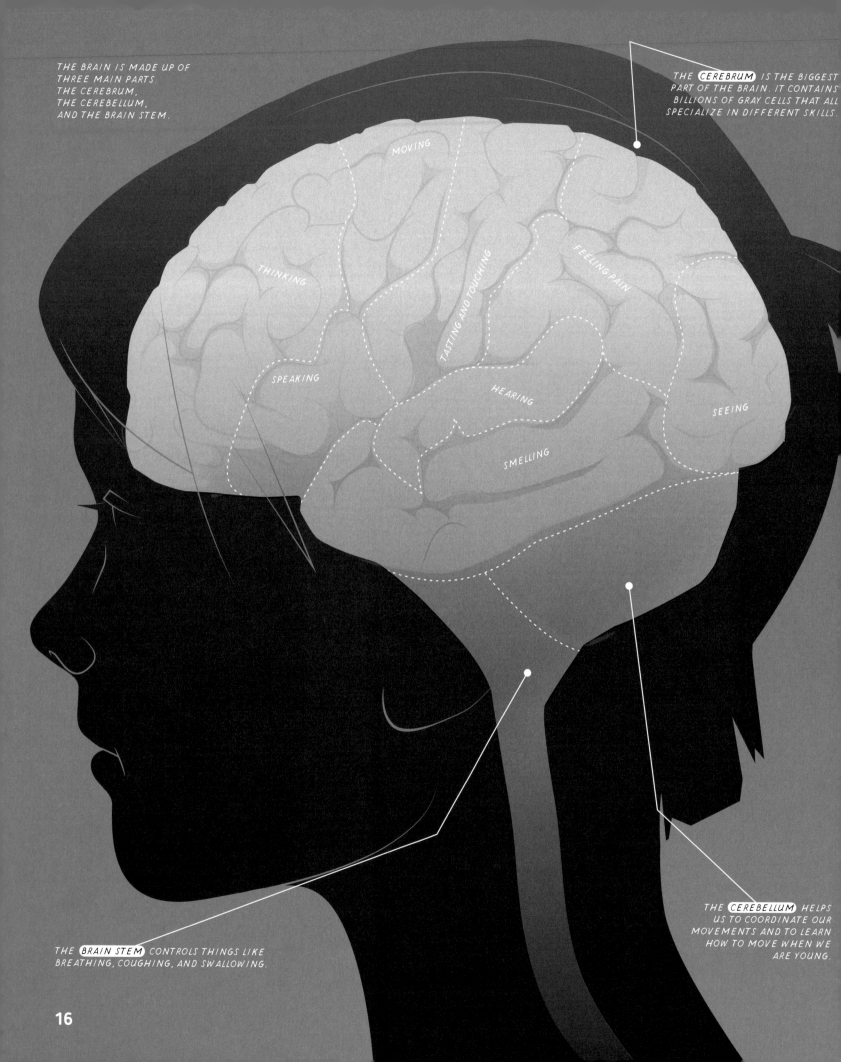

THE BRAIN IS MADE UP OF
THREE MAIN PARTS:
THE CEREBRUM,
THE CEREBELLUM,
AND THE BRAIN STEM.

THE CEREBRUM IS THE BIGGEST
PART OF THE BRAIN. IT CONTAINS
BILLIONS OF GRAY CELLS THAT ALL
SPECIALIZE IN DIFFERENT SKILLS.

MOVING

THINKING

TASTING AND TOUCHING

FEELING PAIN

SPEAKING

HEARING

SEEING

SMELLING

THE CEREBELLUM HELPS
US TO COORDINATE OUR
MOVEMENTS AND TO LEARN
HOW TO MOVE WHEN WE
ARE YOUNG.

THE BRAIN STEM CONTROLS THINGS LIKE
BREATHING, COUGHING, AND SWALLOWING.

16

Smartest Walnut Ever:
THE BRAIN

Do you know anyone who cycles without a helmet? People who do that are playing a dangerous game because they're not protecting one of the most important organs in the body. The brain sits just beneath our skull, so a bike accident with a bare head can leave it injured or damaged. Our brain coordinates everything we do—from walking, talking, and making sandwiches, to playing the piano and learning new words. Different parts of the brain handle different things. Without our cerebellum (which sits in the back), we'd be unable to stand or walk, not to mention balance. Then there's our amygdala, which lives deep inside the brain. Without it, we'd have no fear and would probably start doing really dumb things—like jumping into a campfire and getting badly burned. Our skull is about 0.2 inches thick at the top. We also have three meninges that protect our brain and a liquid that cushions it if we bump our head. The brain itself, which looks like a walnut, weighs about 3.3 pounds in an adult and is 85 percent water. The rest is made up of 100 billion nerve cells that would make any computer green with envy. There's not a laptop in the world that can outperform our brain. It sends electrical signals whizzing around our body and evaluates information it gets from, say, our eyes and ears. It also decides whether we're feeling good or cranky at any given moment. Our brain is always working—even when we're asleep.

A HIPPOPOTAMUS IS SO HEAVY AND SO STRONG THAT IT COULD EASILY FLATTEN US. WHEN IT COMES TO THINKING, THOUGH, WE'RE BETTER EQUIPPED: AT ROUGHLY 1.3 POUNDS, A HIPPO'S BRAIN WEIGHS A LOT LESS THAN OUR 3.3-POUND WALNUT.

THE COCHLEA TRANSFORMS THE VIBRATIONS INTO SIGNALS AND SENDS THEM TO THE AUDITORY NERVE.

SKATEBOARDING WOULD BE HARD WITHOUT OUR VESTIBULAR SYSTEM IT SITS IN THE INNER EAR AND HELPS US KEEP OUR BALANCE.

SOUNDS TRAVEL THROUGH THE AUDITORY CANAL TO THE EARDRUM AND MAKE IT VIBRATE.

THE THING WE USUALLY CALL AN EAR IS REALLY ONLY THE AURICLE IT WORKS LIKE A FUNNEL BY CATCHING SOUNDS AND PASSING THEM ON TO THE ACTUAL EAR.

LISTENING AND SEEING

A Sensitive Listener: The Ear

The ear is made up of more than just the auricle, the part that sticks out on the side of your head. It also contains three little bones that have funny names: hammer, anvil, and stirrup. They are well protected inside our skull because they are super-sensitive and can pick up even the faintest sounds. Everything we hear, whether it's voices, noise, or music, reaches our ears as sound waves. These are invisible ripples that spread out in the air from the source of a noise. They travel into our ear and make the eardrum vibrate, which passes the signal on to the three little bones. They transfer the waves to a liquid in our inner ear. Tiny hair cells then pick up the waves and pass the signals on to the auditory nerve, which carries them to the control center—the brain. Once the brain gets the message, it tells us whether we're hearing a loud holler or beautiful singing. Be careful around loud music and fireworks. If a noise is too loud, it can destroy the delicate hair cells in our inner ear, and those can't grow back once they're gone.

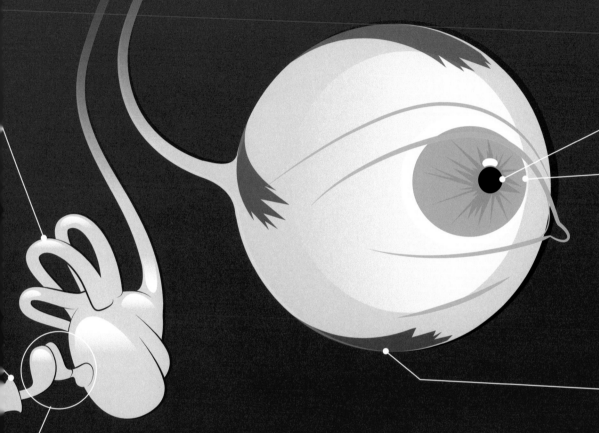

OUR EYES AND EARS USE
NEURAL PATHWAYS TO
SEND SIGNALS FROM THE
OUTSIDE WORLD TO
THE (BRAIN).

LIGHT ENTERS THE EYE
THROUGH THE (PUPIL).

BROWN, BLUE, GREEN, MIXED,
OR SPOTTED: EVERYONE'S (IRISES)
LOOK DIFFERENT. BUT NO MATTER
WHAT THE COLOR, AN IRIS ALWAYS
DOES THE SAME JOB. IT CONTROLS
THE WIDTH OF THE PUPIL AND HOW
MUCH LIGHT ENTERS THE EYE.

(MUSCLES) ARE CONNECTED TO THE
EYE. THEY ALLOW IT TO MOVE SO
THAT WE CAN LOOK IN DIFFERENT
DIRECTIONS.

THREE SMALL BONES ARE LINED UP
BEHIND THE EAR DRUM: (THE HAMMER,
THE ANVIL, AND THE STIRRUP). THEY
RECEIVE VIBRATIONS FROM THE EAR DRUM,
AMPLIFY THEM, AND PASS THEM ON TO THE
COCHLEA.

Better Than Any Camera: The Eye

Our eyes are world champs at focusing. It would be pretty frustrating if we had to press a zoom button before we could spot a bird's nest up a tree! Our eye muscles move up to 100,000 times per day to allow us to see clearly. If you have a good set of eyes, you'll be able to see about 10 million different shades of color. Strangely enough, eyes can't actually see. They just receive (light stimuli) and send these along the optic nerve to the brain, which decodes the information and puts the picture together.

SMELLING AND TASTING

Smell and taste are two of the body's five senses. They differ from the other three because they are chemical. This means our body's receptors can pick up tiny, invisible odor particles in the air and in our food. By working together, these two senses allow us to experience every aspect of a taste.

WE ARE SURROUNDED BY ALL SORTS OF SMELLS. WHEN YOU BREATHE, YOU INHALE AIR THAT BRINGS MOLECULES OF THOSE SMELLS INTO YOUR NOSE.

THIS IS THE OLFACTORY BULB.

THE OLFACTORY EPITHELIUM IS THE SIZE OF A POSTAGE STAMP AND SITS IN THE ROOF OF THE NASAL CAVITY. ODOR MOLECULES DOCK ONTO ITS RECEPTOR CELLS, WHICH TRANSMIT THE SIGNALS TO THE BRAIN VIA THE OLFACTORY BULB.

A Specialist Sniffer: The Nose

Our nose allows us to breathe, obviously. But it also warms up the air for our lungs and cleans it. The air is full of invisible dirt. If you want evidence, think about how boogers are usually greenish-gray. That's from all the dirt floating around. Boogers would be see-through if the air was clean. When you have a stuffy nose, you can still breathe through your mouth. But just try enjoying a fresh slice of apple pie with a cold. It won't work because our sense of taste only functions properly if we can smell. Our brain is really good at storing memories of smells, which is why they can remind us of things that happened in the past. Almost everyone can tell the difference between about 4,000 different smells, but experts like wine connoisseurs and perfume specialists can pick out more than 10,000. There's no need to feel envious, though, those talented noses will also be super sensitive to gross smells!

The Tongue

If you look in the mirror and stick out your tongue, you'll see it's covered in nipples. Yes, you read that right! The tiny bumps on your tongue are called papillae, which comes from the Latin word for nipples. Each papilla is home to between 1 and 200 taste buds so our sense of taste depends on them. Some buds specialize in sweet tastes, while others focus on the bitter, sour, salty, or umami (a Japanese word that means savory or meaty). Try putting a piece of candy in the middle of your tongue and see how it tastes. Our tongue is also crucial for speech. Without it, we wouldn't be able to make the sounds that form words. We also need a tongue for kissing and eating. It would be really hard to chew food minus a tongue. Our tongue moves the food around as we chew and pushes it towards our esophagus when we're ready to swallow.

THE TONGUE HAS DIFFERENT AREAS FOR EACH OF THE FIVE BASIC TASTES.

SIGNALS FROM THE OLFACTORY RECEPTORS AND TASTE RECEPTORS COME TOGETHER IN THE BRAIN TO CREATE A COMPLETE TASTE SENSATION.

THE TONGUE IS COVERED WITH TASTE RECEPTOR CELLS.

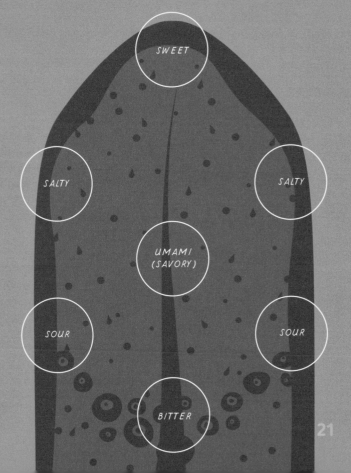

SWEET

SALTY

SALTY

UMAMI
(SAVORY)

SOUR

SOUR

BITTER

21

THE ❲UVULA❳ ISN'T JUST HANGING AROUND AT THE BACK OF YOUR
MOUTH FOR NO REASON. WHEN FOOD TOUCHES IT AS WE SWALLOW,
THE UVULA MAKES SURE WE DON'T CHOKE ON WHAT WE'RE EATING.
SOME LANGUAGES ALSO USE IT TO MAKE SOUNDS FOR CERTAIN WORDS.

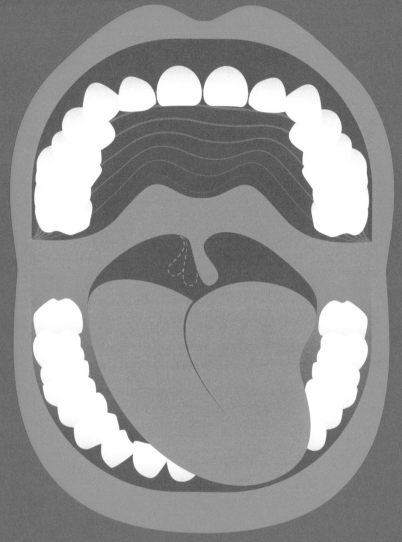

THE ORAL CAVITY IS LINED WITH A MUCOUS MEMBRANE. THE SALIVARY
GLANDS, WHICH PRODUCE ❲SALIVA,❳ SIT UNDERNEATH THE TONGUE, WAY
BACK IN YOUR MOUTH, CLOSE TO YOUR EARS.

A Watery All-Rounder: The Mouth

Your mouth lets you do lots of neat stuff: eat, drink, taste, kiss, pull faces. When you're hungry
or eating, your mouth gets really watery. Sometimes just hearing about food is enough to
make your ❲salivary glands❳ open up. We produce about 34 ounces of saliva (or spit) every day.
Saliva is pretty much all water, but the other ingredients pack quite a punch. Over 10 billion
bacteria swim around in our mouths, thriving on the food we eat or even chewing holes in
our teeth! So a mouth isn't a clean place—and it can also get pretty stinky, like after we've
been asleep and haven't eaten or drunk anything for a long time. Cleaning your teeth and
eating breakfast will fix the problem. If you get garlic breath, though, the smell doesn't only
come from your mouth or even from your stomach. It also comes from your intestines! They
absorb the smell and pass it on to your blood.

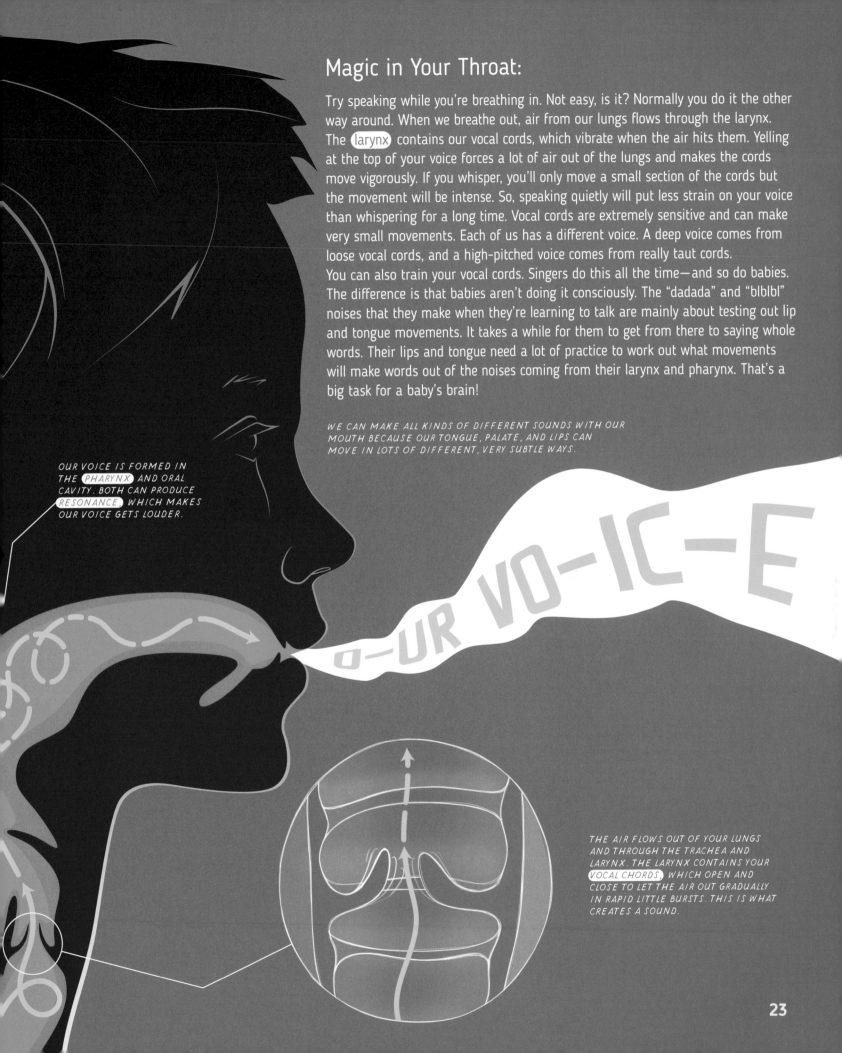

Magic in Your Throat:

Try speaking while you're breathing in. Not easy, is it? Normally you do it the other way around. When we breathe out, air from our lungs flows through the larynx. The ⟨larynx⟩ contains our vocal cords, which vibrate when the air hits them. Yelling at the top of your voice forces a lot of air out of the lungs and makes the cords move vigorously. If you whisper, you'll only move a small section of the cords but the movement will be intense. So, speaking quietly will put less strain on your voice than whispering for a long time. Vocal cords are extremely sensitive and can make very small movements. Each of us has a different voice. A deep voice comes from loose vocal cords, and a high-pitched voice comes from really taut cords.

You can also train your vocal cords. Singers do this all the time—and so do babies. The difference is that babies aren't doing it consciously. The "dadada" and "blblbl" noises that they make when they're learning to talk are mainly about testing out lip and tongue movements. It takes a while for them to get from there to saying whole words. Their lips and tongue need a lot of practice to work out what movements will make words out of the noises coming from their larynx and pharynx. That's a big task for a baby's brain!

WE CAN MAKE ALL KINDS OF DIFFERENT SOUNDS WITH OUR MOUTH BECAUSE OUR TONGUE, PALATE, AND LIPS CAN MOVE IN LOTS OF DIFFERENT, VERY SUBTLE WAYS.

OUR VOICE IS FORMED IN THE ⟨PHARYNX⟩ AND ORAL CAVITY. BOTH CAN PRODUCE ⟨RESONANCE,⟩ WHICH MAKES OUR VOICE GETS LOUDER.

THE AIR FLOWS OUT OF YOUR LUNGS AND THROUGH THE TRACHEA AND LARYNX. THE LARYNX CONTAINS YOUR ⟨VOCAL CHORDS,⟩ WHICH OPEN AND CLOSE TO LET THE AIR OUT GRADUALLY IN RAPID LITTLE BURSTS. THIS IS WHAT CREATES A SOUND.

Protective and Flaky:
THE SKIN

Yum! Your skin tastes so good! At least that's what all the little bugs that feed on it think. Microscopic dust mites that live all over your house—in your bed, in the carpet, on the couch—just love eating tiny flakes of skin. And because your skin sheds dead skin cells all the time, the mites have a never-ending supply of snacks. Even the dust you find on bookshelves is made up almost entirely of dead skin. This is normal and it doesn't mean you need to take a shower every 10 minutes. Washing only kills off the good bacteria, and your skin grows back anyway. If you wash too often, the skin's own protective film can become too thin and germs might start getting in. Keeping your skin healthy is really important. As the biggest organ in the human body, it protects us from dirt and stops us from drying out. Do you have a birthmark? Maybe more than one? Birthmarks are brownish splotches that some people have on their skin. They can be big or small, and you have them from birth. That's where the name comes from. Moles are similar to birthmarks. They are often invisible when you're young and only develop later in life. A substance called melanin is responsible for making dark moles and birthmarks. The sun can also cause moles to appear. Look after your skin in the sun by wearing lots of sunscreen and covering up. If you do have a mole, get your doctor to check it out. He or she might refer you to a derma-tologist for a closer look. One last thing: did you know that, just like the irises in our eyes, we all have totally unique skin? Your fingerprint has an unmistakable pattern that belongs just to you.

OUR SKIN HAS LOTS OF DIFFERENT JOBS TO DO. FOR INSTANCE, IT ALLOWS US TO TOUCH THINGS AND PROTECTS THE TISSUE UNDERNEATH.

Super Sensitive: Touch

Without nerves and their lightning-quick connection to the brain, our skin would not be able to sense the things that happen to it. Thankfully, the skin is full of nerves that can all feel very different things. Really faint sensations are picked up by the hairs on your skin. Their roots are connected to nerves that send the stimulus to the brain. Your sense of touch is not equally strong everywhere, though. Your cheeks, lips, the soles of your feet, and, above all, the palms of your hands and your finger-tips are the best at feeling. The ridges on your fingertips are much more sensitive to touch than your eyes are to the world around you. The skin on your thighs and the back of your knees is not especially sensitive. So if a bee has to sting you, it should sting you there!

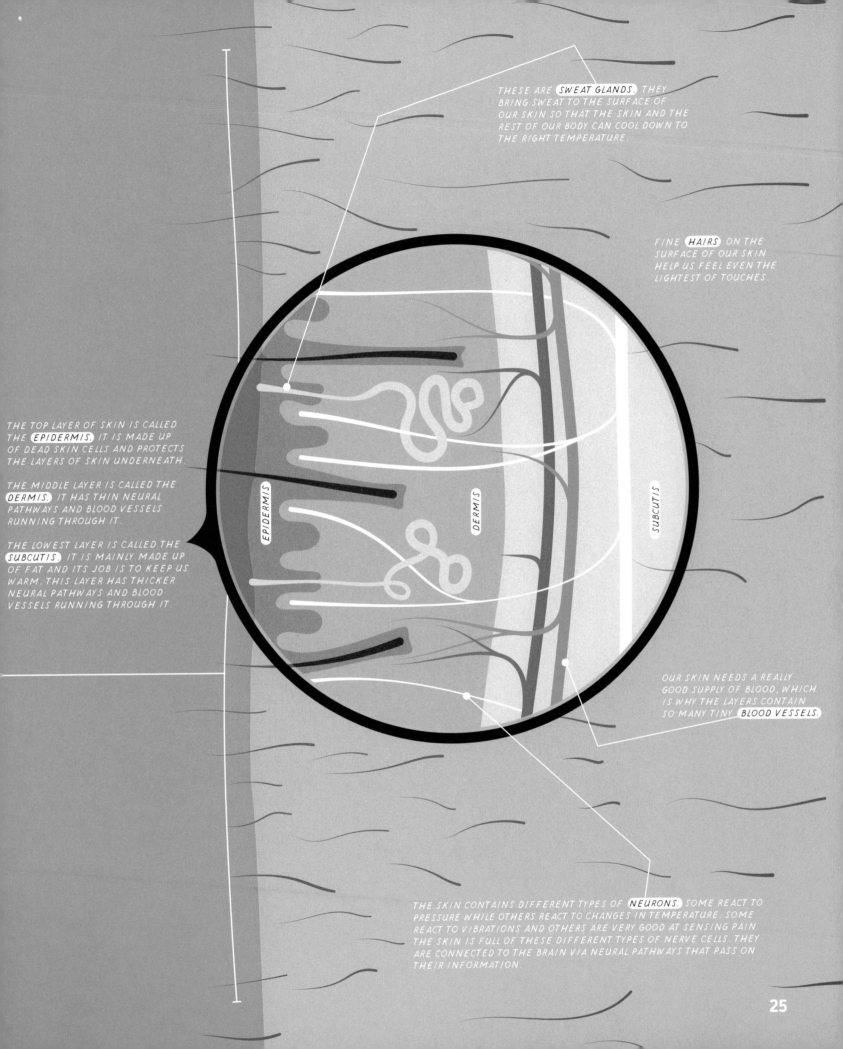

THESE ARE SWEAT GLANDS. THEY BRING SWEAT TO THE SURFACE OF OUR SKIN SO THAT THE SKIN AND THE REST OF OUR BODY CAN COOL DOWN TO THE RIGHT TEMPERATURE.

FINE HAIRS ON THE SURFACE OF OUR SKIN HELP US FEEL EVEN THE LIGHTEST OF TOUCHES.

THE TOP LAYER OF SKIN IS CALLED THE EPIDERMIS. IT IS MADE UP OF DEAD SKIN CELLS AND PROTECTS THE LAYERS OF SKIN UNDERNEATH.

THE MIDDLE LAYER IS CALLED THE DERMIS. IT HAS THIN NEURAL PATHWAYS AND BLOOD VESSELS RUNNING THROUGH IT.

THE LOWEST LAYER IS CALLED THE SUBCUTIS. IT IS MAINLY MADE UP OF FAT AND ITS JOB IS TO KEEP US WARM. THIS LAYER HAS THICKER NEURAL PATHWAYS AND BLOOD VESSELS RUNNING THROUGH IT.

EPIDERMIS

DERMIS

SUBCUTIS

OUR SKIN NEEDS A REALLY GOOD SUPPLY OF BLOOD, WHICH IS WHY THE LAYERS CONTAIN SO MANY TINY BLOOD VESSELS.

THE SKIN CONTAINS DIFFERENT TYPES OF NEURONS. SOME REACT TO PRESSURE WHILE OTHERS REACT TO CHANGES IN TEMPERATURE. SOME REACT TO VIBRATIONS AND OTHERS ARE VERY GOOD AT SENSING PAIN. THE SKIN IS FULL OF THESE DIFFERENT TYPES OF NERVE CELLS. THEY ARE CONNECTED TO THE BRAIN VIA NEURAL PATHWAYS THAT PASS ON THEIR INFORMATION.

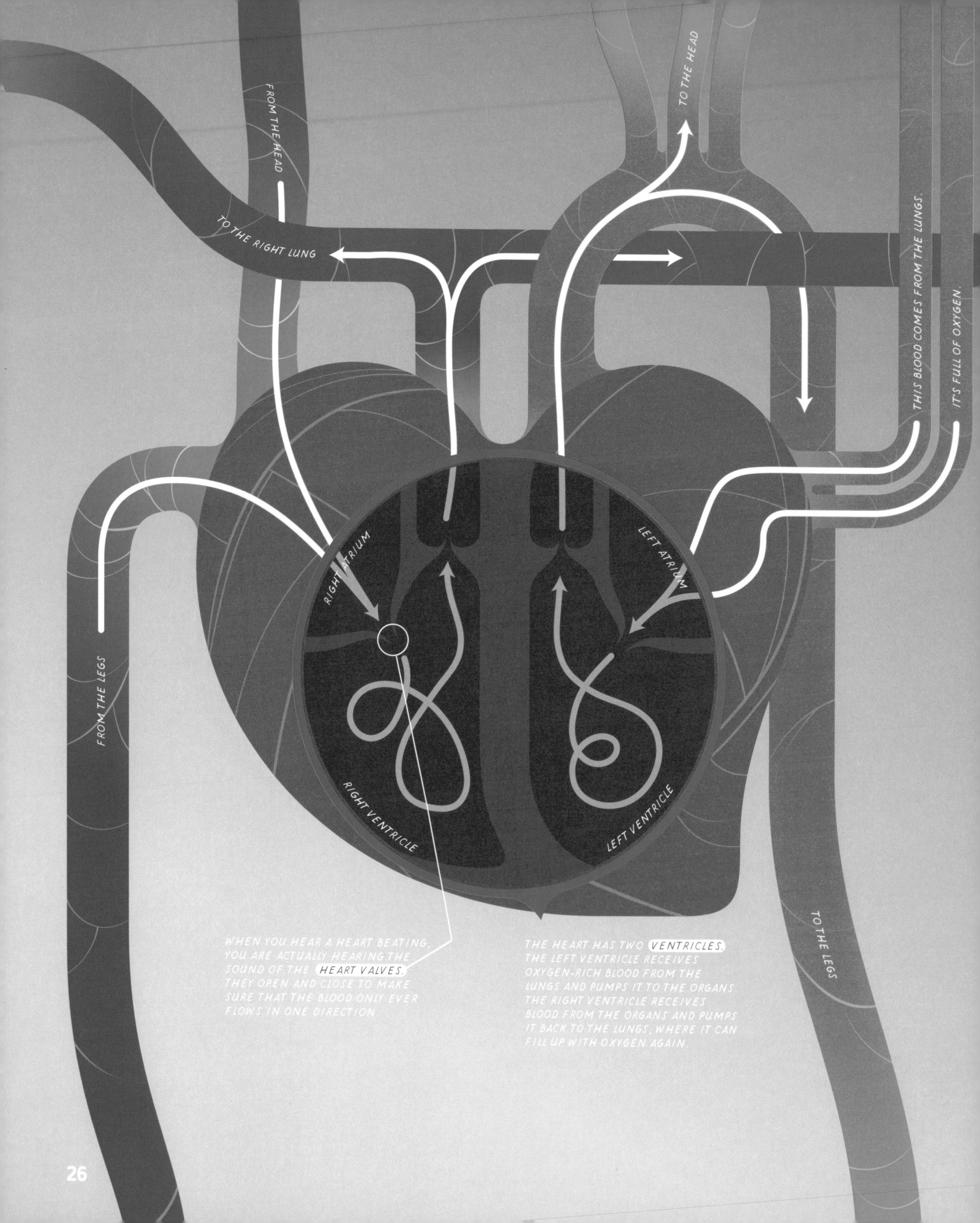

FROM THE HEAD

TO THE RIGHT LUNG

TO THE HEAD

THIS BLOOD COMES FROM THE LUNGS.

IT'S FULL OF OXYGEN

RIGHT ATRIUM

LEFT ATRIUM

FROM THE LEGS

RIGHT VENTRICLE

LEFT VENTRICLE

TO THE LEGS

WHEN YOU HEAR A HEART BEATING, YOU ARE ACTUALLY HEARING THE SOUND OF THE HEART VALVES. THEY OPEN AND CLOSE TO MAKE SURE THAT THE BLOOD ONLY EVER FLOWS IN ONE DIRECTION

THE HEART HAS TWO VENTRICLES. THE LEFT VENTRICLE RECEIVES OXYGEN-RICH BLOOD FROM THE LUNGS AND PUMPS IT TO THE ORGANS. THE RIGHT VENTRICLE RECEIVES BLOOD FROM THE ORGANS AND PUMPS IT BACK TO THE LUNGS, WHERE IT CAN FILL UP WITH OXYGEN AGAIN.

A Pump That Never Sleeps:
THE HEART

Blood flows into the lungs, fills up on oxygen, flows into the heart, flows back out again, travels around the body, delivers oxygen to the cells, returns to the heart, then back to the lungs to fill up with oxygen ... This is how our (circulatory system) works. It happens very quickly and repeats itself over and over. The heart pumps all the blood (in adults, that's about 10 pints) around the body in about a minute. The blood always takes the same route. It flows out of the heart, through blood vessels known as arteries, and on to our organs and cells. It doesn't do it voluntarily, though: every time your heart beats, it forces your blood to keep moving forward. The body's biggest (artery) is the aorta, which carries oxygen-rich blood that travels through smaller arteries to reach our chest, arms, legs, and head. When blood enters the (capillaries,) it unloads its oxygen and flows into our veins. (Veins) are also blood vessels, but, unlike the arteries, their job is to carry blood back to the heart.

1 THE BLOOD BEGINS BY FLOWING INTO THE LEFT ATRIUM AND THE RIGHT ATRIUM. THIS CAUSES BOTH ATRIA TO EXPAND A LITTLE.

2 THE HEART VALVES OPEN, ALLOWING THE BLOOD TO FLOW FROM THE ATRIA INTO THE VENTRICLES. THE ATRIA BECOME SMALLER.

3 NOW THE VENTRICLES ARE FILLED WITH BLOOD, WHICH HAS MADE THEM A LOT BIGGER.

4 THE VENTRICLES THEN CONTRACT AND PUMP THE BLOOD OUT THROUGH THE VALVES.

You probably know what it sounds and feels like when your heart beats really fast, right? Like when you play sports. There's nothing to worry about when that happens. In fact, it's really good for you because exercise makes your heart stronger. Just like any other muscle, your heart needs regular workouts so that it can keep doing its job well as you grow older. Your heart works especially hard when you're doing sports—in other words, it beats faster and harder. This is because it has to pump more blood to your muscles, which need a lot more oxygen than usual. When you're relaxing on the couch, your heartbeat will be really relaxed because your body only needs a normal amount of blood. Even so, about two pints of blood flow through your brain every minute. Plus, even when we're not moving, the cells in our body still need oxygen to keep on living. That's why your heart never stops pumping. The resting heart rate in humans is about 130 beats per minute for a baby, 100 beats per minute for a child, and 70 beats per minute for an adult. You can feel your pulse by touching the underside of your wrist.

Inhale, Exhale, Repeat:
THE LUNGS

We inhale and exhale about 25,000 times per day. Breathing is totally automatic and we mostly do it through our nose. We really only notice our breathing if we get a stuffy nose and have to start using our mouth to get air into our trachea. The trachea is a tube that splits off into two branches called bronchi. These then divide into loads of really tiny tubes called bronchioles. They take air to tiny sacs called alveoli—there are over 150 million of these in each lung. Once air gets into the alveoli, a big trade-off happens. The alveoli are surrounded by a thin network of blood vessels, which allows them to send fresh oxygen into the blood. In return, they absorb the waste gas (carbon dioxide) from the low-oxygen blood that the heart pumps to them. We get rid of the carbon dioxide when we exhale. Without this exchange, we'd suffocate. That's why we have to breathe and why we can only hold our breath for a short time. The longer we hold our breath—by staying underwater, for example—the more carbon dioxide builds up in our blood and our cells. If necessary, our brain triggers a reflex that forces us to breathe so that we can top up on oxygen and get rid of carbon dioxide.

FOR BREATHING, WE RELY ON ONE MUSCLE MORE THAN ANY OTHER: THE DIAPHRAGM, WHICH SITS JUST UNDER OUR LUNGS. WHEN IT CONTRACTS, OUR LUNGS EXPAND, AND WE INHALE. WHEN IT RELAXES, IT FORCES THE LUNGS UPWARDS AGAIN, AND WE EXHALE.

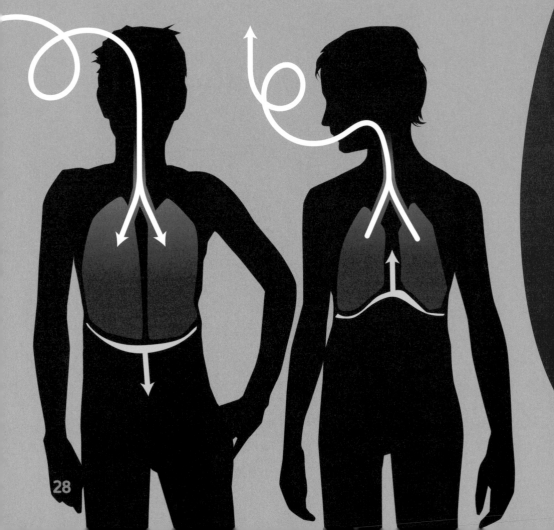

RIGHT LUNG

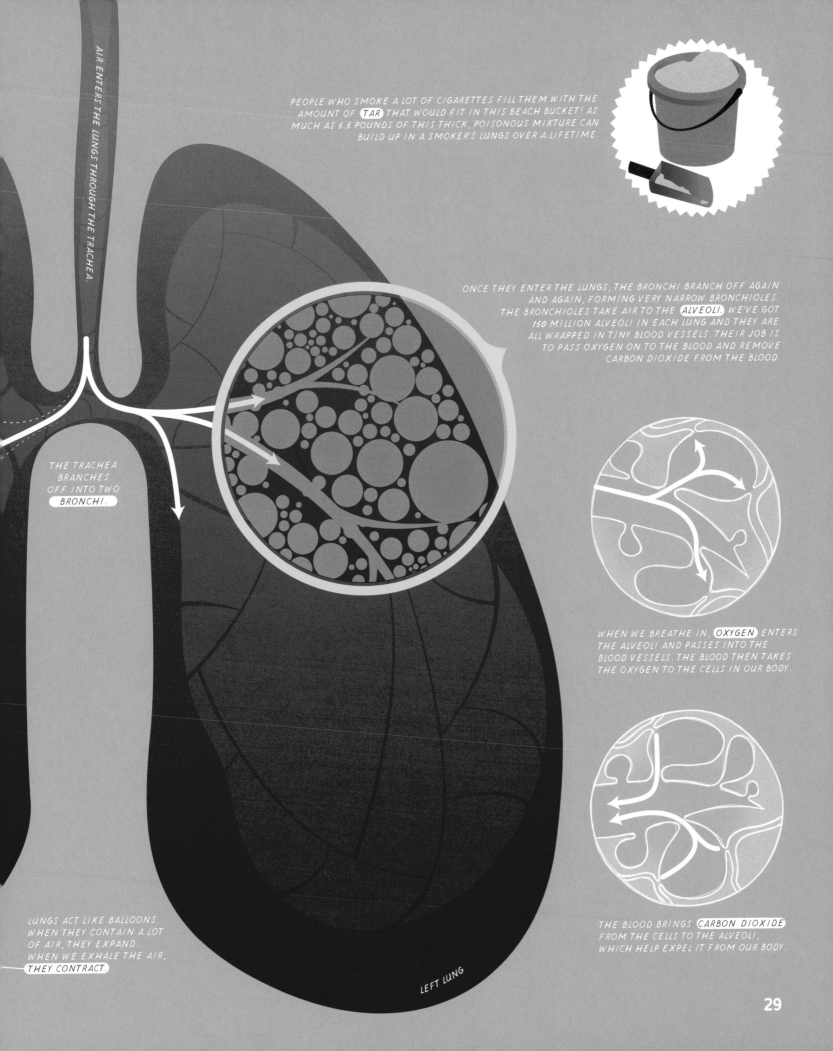

AIR ENTERS THE LUNGS THROUGH THE TRACHEA.

PEOPLE WHO SMOKE A LOT OF CIGARETTES FILL THEM WITH THE AMOUNT OF TAR THAT WOULD FIT IN THIS BEACH BUCKET! AS MUCH AS 5.5 POUNDS OF THIS THICK, POISONOUS MIXTURE CAN BUILD UP IN A SMOKER'S LUNGS OVER A LIFETIME.

ONCE THEY ENTER THE LUNGS, THE BRONCHI BRANCH OFF AGAIN AND AGAIN, FORMING VERY NARROW BRONCHIOLES. THE BRONCHIOLES TAKE AIR TO THE ALVEOLI. WE'VE GOT 150 MILLION ALVEOLI IN EACH LUNG AND THEY ARE ALL WRAPPED IN TINY BLOOD VESSELS. THEIR JOB IS TO PASS OXYGEN ON TO THE BLOOD AND REMOVE CARBON DIOXIDE FROM THE BLOOD.

THE TRACHEA BRANCHES OFF INTO TWO BRONCHI.

WHEN WE BREATHE IN, OXYGEN ENTERS THE ALVEOLI AND PASSES INTO THE BLOOD VESSELS. THE BLOOD THEN TAKES THE OXYGEN TO THE CELLS IN OUR BODY.

LUNGS ACT LIKE BALLOONS. WHEN THEY CONTAIN A LOT OF AIR, THEY EXPAND. WHEN WE EXHALE THE AIR, THEY CONTRACT.

THE BLOOD BRINGS CARBON DIOXIDE FROM THE CELLS TO THE ALVEOLI, WHICH HELP EXPEL IT FROM OUR BODY.

LEFT LUNG

29

A Vital Delivery Service:
THE BLOOD

Blood is always on the move. Even if we're in a deep sleep, it just keeps on flowing around and around our body. As blood travels, it supplies our cells with everything they need. The most important cargo of all is oxygen. Every single cell in the human body—from our fingertips to our feet—needs oxygen to keep functioning. Without it, our cells would shut down and we'd be dead within minutes. Blood is red because a single drop contains about 5 million red blood cells, whose job it is to store oxygen. That same drop of blood also contains about 9,000 white blood cells. These are crucial because they help you get better when you're sick. Blood platelets—about 270,000 per drop—are also important. They stop us from bleeding and heal the wound if we cut ourselves. Half of our blood is made up of a yellowish liquid called plasma. Plasma is water that has nutrients in it. The blood takes these nutrients to our cells. The blood also picks up the waste that our cells produce, which is why it keeps having to visit the kidneys for a wash.

IF YOU TIED ALL THE BLOOD VESSELS IN YOUR BODY TOGETHER, THEY WOULD STRETCH FOR ABOUT *62,000* MILES. THAT'S LONG ENOUGH TO WRAP AROUND THE WORLD *2.5* TIMES!

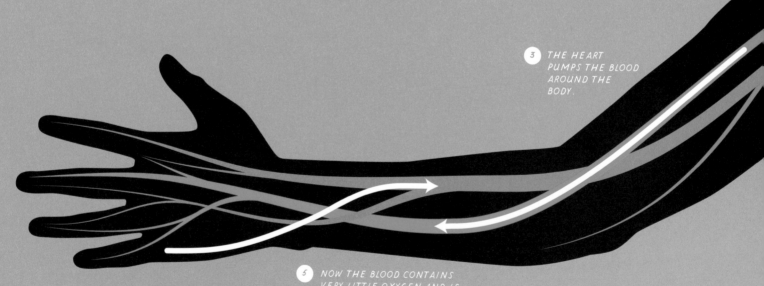

3 THE HEART PUMPS THE BLOOD AROUND THE BODY.

4 BLOOD ENTERS THE CELLS VIA THE CAPILLARIES, WHICH ARE THE THINNEST BLOOD VESSELS OF ALL. IN FACT, CAPILLARIES ARE SO THIN THAT YOU CAN'T SEE THEM WITH THE NAKED EYE. THEY EXIST EVERYWHERE IN THE BODY.

5 NOW THE BLOOD CONTAINS VERY LITTLE OXYGEN AND IS SENT BACK TO THE HEART.

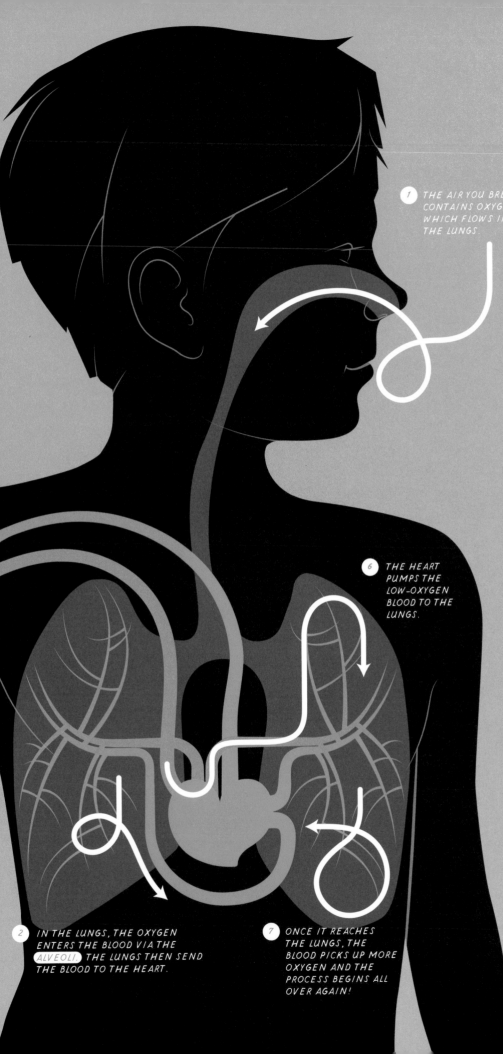

YOUR BODY CONTAINS LARGE AND SMALL BLOOD VESSELS THAT BRING BLOOD FROM THE HEART TO EVERY CELL IN YOUR BODY.

① THE AIR YOU BREATHE CONTAINS OXYGEN, WHICH FLOWS INTO THE LUNGS.

⑥ THE HEART PUMPS THE LOW-OXYGEN BLOOD TO THE LUNGS.

② IN THE LUNGS, THE OXYGEN ENTERS THE BLOOD VIA THE ALVEOLI. THE LUNGS THEN SEND THE BLOOD TO THE HEART.

⑦ ONCE IT REACHES THE LUNGS, THE BLOOD PICKS UP MORE OXYGEN AND THE PROCESS BEGINS ALL OVER AGAIN!

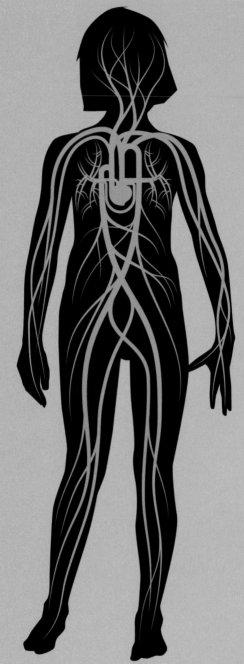

CAPILLARIES ALLOW OXYGEN TO PASS FROM THE BLOOD AND INTO THE CELLS. THIS IS WHY WE HAVE TWO TYPES OF BLOOD IN OUR BODY.

OXYGEN-RICH BLOOD FLOWS TO THE CELLS THROUGH THE RED VESSELS.

LOW-OXYGEN BLOOD FLOWS AWAY FROM THE CELLS THROUGH THE BLUE VESSELS.

31

Internal Band-Aids:
HEALING

Ouch! Falling over and getting a bloody knee is no fun. But it won't bleed for long because (platelets) rush to the scene and start collecting in the wound. Red blood cells get caught up in them and plug up the cut so that no more blood can get out and no more dirt can get in. As the plug dries, it forms a scab, which is a natural Band-Aid. The blood vessels underneath can heal in peace, and your skin can grow back over the cut. Even if you stop thinking about your fall after a few minutes, your body sure doesn't. While you get on with your day, your blood sends a whole army of phagocytes to the cut. (Phagocytes) are cells that attack and kill any nasty bacteria that have found their way into the wound. If they win, the cut won't get infected. If the bacteria triumph, it will fill with pus. Gross! Not to worry, though: your body can usually fix that, too.

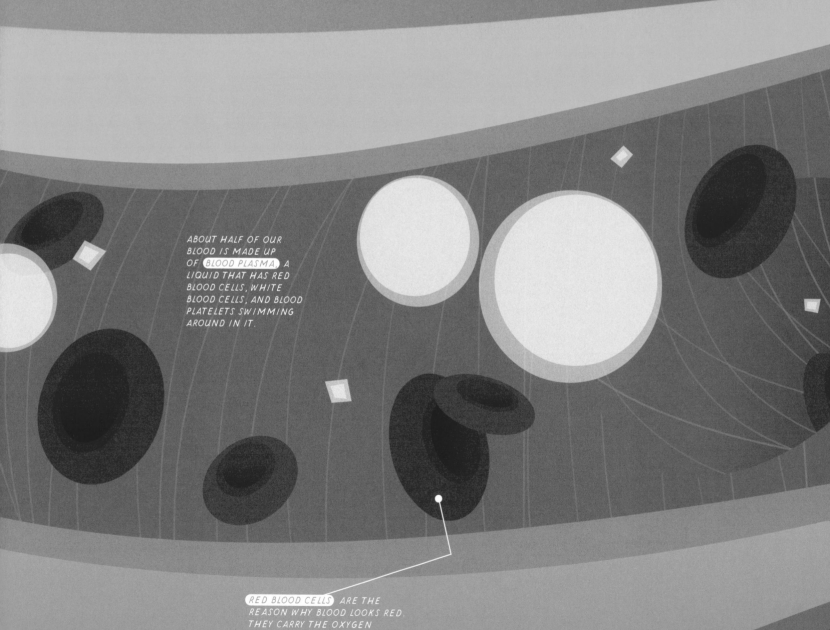

ABOUT HALF OF OUR BLOOD IS MADE UP OF (BLOOD PLASMA,) A LIQUID THAT HAS RED BLOOD CELLS, WHITE BLOOD CELLS, AND BLOOD PLATELETS SWIMMING AROUND IN IT.

(RED BLOOD CELLS) ARE THE REASON WHY BLOOD LOOKS RED. THEY CARRY THE OXYGEN THAT THE BLOOD DELIVERS TO THE CELLS IN OUR BODY.

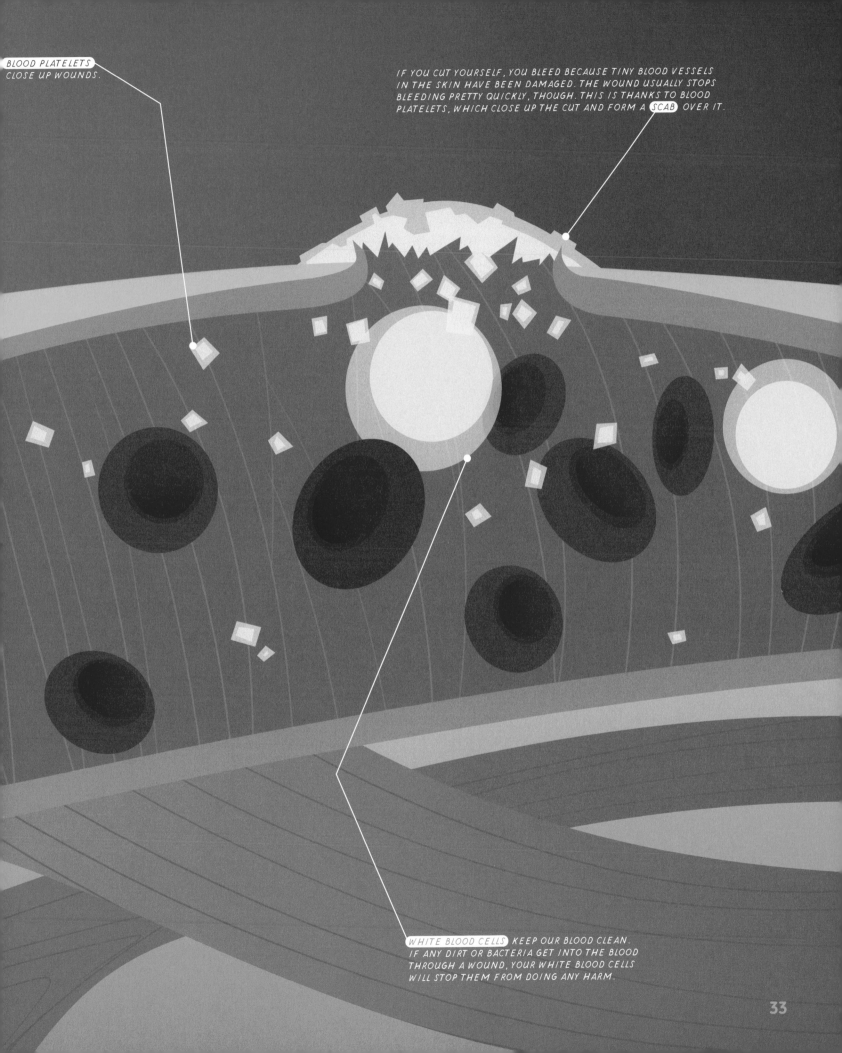

BLOOD PLATELETS
CLOSE UP WOUNDS.

IF YOU CUT YOURSELF, YOU BLEED BECAUSE TINY BLOOD VESSELS
IN THE SKIN HAVE BEEN DAMAGED. THE WOUND USUALLY STOPS
BLEEDING PRETTY QUICKLY, THOUGH. THIS IS THANKS TO BLOOD
PLATELETS, WHICH CLOSE UP THE CUT AND FORM A SCAB OVER IT.

WHITE BLOOD CELLS KEEP OUR BLOOD CLEAN.
IF ANY DIRT OR BACTERIA GET INTO THE BLOOD
THROUGH A WOUND, YOUR WHITE BLOOD CELLS
WILL STOP THEM FROM DOING ANY HARM.

A Superhero Factory:
THE IMMUNE SYSTEM

LYMPHOCYTES (B-CELLS AND T-CELLS) ARE MADE IN THE BONES. B-CELLS PRODUCE PLASMA CELLS, WHICH SCOUT OUT VIRUSES AND PRODUCE ANTIBODIES.

Did you know your blood is full of superheroes?! Even though white blood cells are microscopic and don't wear masks or capes, they really do have super powers. The cells swim around in your blood and lymph. Lymph is a thick fluid that surrounds every cell in the body. Some white blood cells produce antibodies to ward off bacteria and viruses. Others kill invaders by eating them. The lymph picks up the dead germs and other cell waste and deposits it in your lymph nodes (we've got about 500 to 600 of each of these). The really neat thing is that the superheroes can remember who they killed in the past. If the same thing attacks again, your body can react much faster and make the right kind of antibodies.

AFTER THE CIRCULATORY SYSTEM, THE BODY'S MOST IMPORTANT TRANSPORT NETWORK IS THE LYMPHATIC SYSTEM. LYMPH IS A FLUID THAT OCCURS WHEN BLOOD PLASMA LEAKS THROUGH CAPILLARIES AND INTO THE BODY'S TISSUE. LYMPH IS FILTERED IN THE LYMPH NODES AND THEN RETURNS TO THE CIRCULATORY SYSTEM—RIGHT HERE

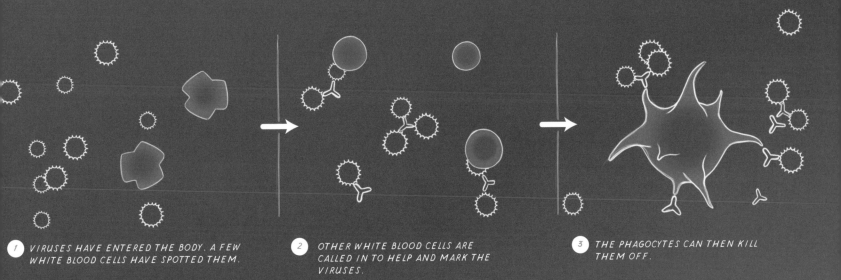

1   VIRUSES HAVE ENTERED THE BODY. A FEW WHITE BLOOD CELLS HAVE SPOTTED THEM.

2   OTHER WHITE BLOOD CELLS ARE CALLED IN TO HELP AND MARK THE VIRUSES.

3   THE PHAGOCYTES CAN THEN KILL THEM OFF.

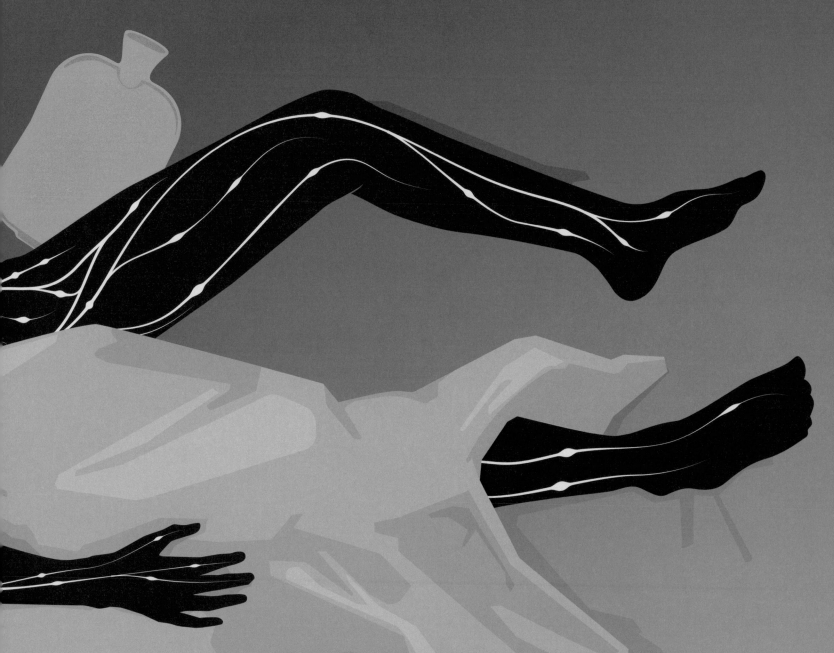

Mix and Match: The Food We Eat

Potato chips and chocolate taste so good! But if we only ate chips and chocolate, we'd get sick. For a start, chocolate is bad for your teeth, but that's not the end of the story. Junk food doesn't contain all the substances that the body needs in order to stay healthy. To make sure you can keep running around the backyard and playing soccer, you have to eat a balanced, varied diet. That's the only way to give your body what it needs.

THE RIGHT MIX OF NUTRIENTS GIVES US ENERGY AND ALLOWS OUR BODY TO GROW AND STAY STRONG.

CARBOHYDRATES

PROTEIN

FATS

WATER, MINERALS, FIBER, AND VITAMINS HELP STOP US FROM GETTING SICK. THEY ALSO LOOK AFTER OUR ORGANS AND ENSURE THAT THE BODY'S MANY DIFFERENT FUNCTIONS KEEP RUNNING SMOOTHLY.

SALT

FIBER

VITAMINS

TRACE ELEMENTS AND MINERALS

PHYTOCHEMICALS

WATER

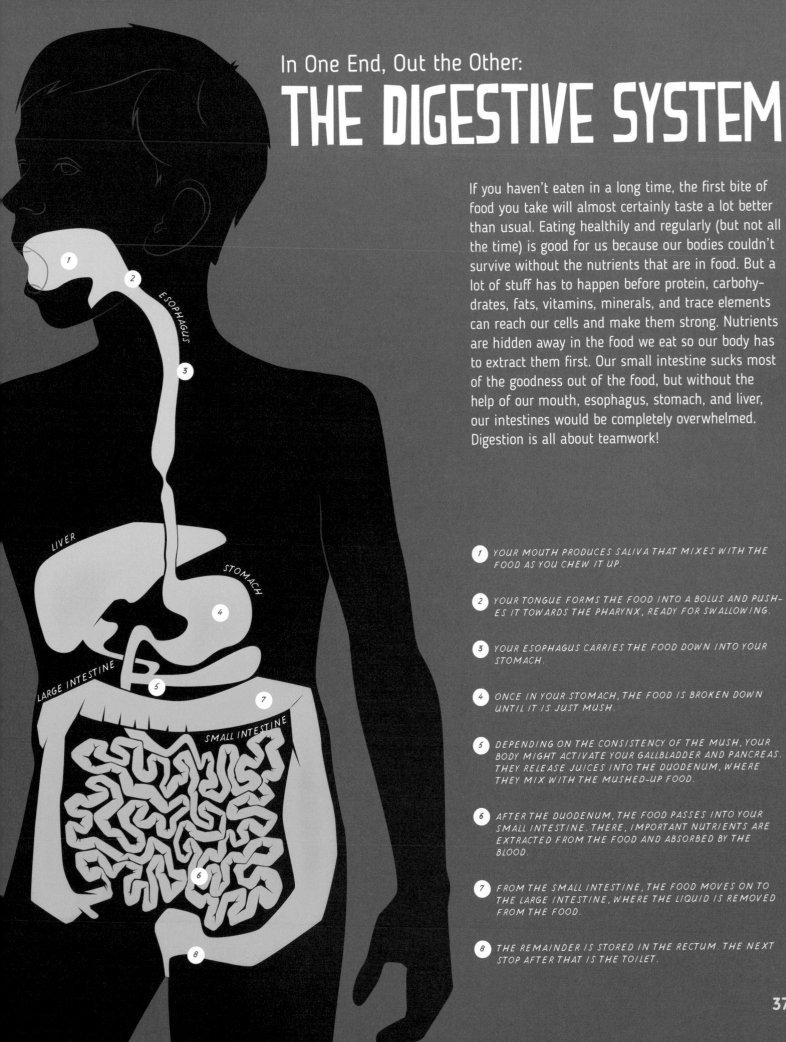

In One End, Out the Other:
THE DIGESTIVE SYSTEM

If you haven't eaten in a long time, the first bite of food you take will almost certainly taste a lot better than usual. Eating healthily and regularly (but not all the time) is good for us because our bodies couldn't survive without the nutrients that are in food. But a lot of stuff has to happen before protein, carbohydrates, fats, vitamins, minerals, and trace elements can reach our cells and make them strong. Nutrients are hidden away in the food we eat so our body has to extract them first. Our small intestine sucks most of the goodness out of the food, but without the help of our mouth, esophagus, stomach, and liver, our intestines would be completely overwhelmed. Digestion is all about teamwork!

ESOPHAGUS

LIVER

STOMACH

LARGE INTESTINE

SMALL INTESTINE

(1) YOUR MOUTH PRODUCES SALIVA THAT MIXES WITH THE FOOD AS YOU CHEW IT UP.

(2) YOUR TONGUE FORMS THE FOOD INTO A BOLUS AND PUSHES IT TOWARDS THE PHARYNX, READY FOR SWALLOWING.

(3) YOUR ESOPHAGUS CARRIES THE FOOD DOWN INTO YOUR STOMACH.

(4) ONCE IN YOUR STOMACH, THE FOOD IS BROKEN DOWN UNTIL IT IS JUST MUSH.

(5) DEPENDING ON THE CONSISTENCY OF THE MUSH, YOUR BODY MIGHT ACTIVATE YOUR GALLBLADDER AND PANCREAS. THEY RELEASE JUICES INTO THE DUODENUM, WHERE THEY MIX WITH THE MUSHED-UP FOOD.

(6) AFTER THE DUODENUM, THE FOOD PASSES INTO YOUR SMALL INTESTINE. THERE, IMPORTANT NUTRIENTS ARE EXTRACTED FROM THE FOOD AND ABSORBED BY THE BLOOD.

(7) FROM THE SMALL INTESTINE, THE FOOD MOVES ON TO THE LARGE INTESTINE, WHERE THE LIQUID IS REMOVED FROM THE FOOD.

(8) THE REMAINDER IS STORED IN THE RECTUM. THE NEXT STOP AFTER THAT IS THE TOILET.

First Stop: The Mouth, Teeth, and Esophagus

The better you chew your food, the easier life will be for your stomach. Plus, good chewing can turn even the toughest slice of pumpernickel into a sweet treat. That's because your saliva converts the starch in the bread into sugar. So don't wolf things down! A good dose of saliva will also help food slide smoothly through the esophagus. The (esophagus) isn't a rigid tube. It's made of muscle that contracts to move chewed-up food into the stomach. It also has a kind of hatch that shuts the entrance to the stomach when we're not using it—otherwise everything would fall out whenever we did a headstand!

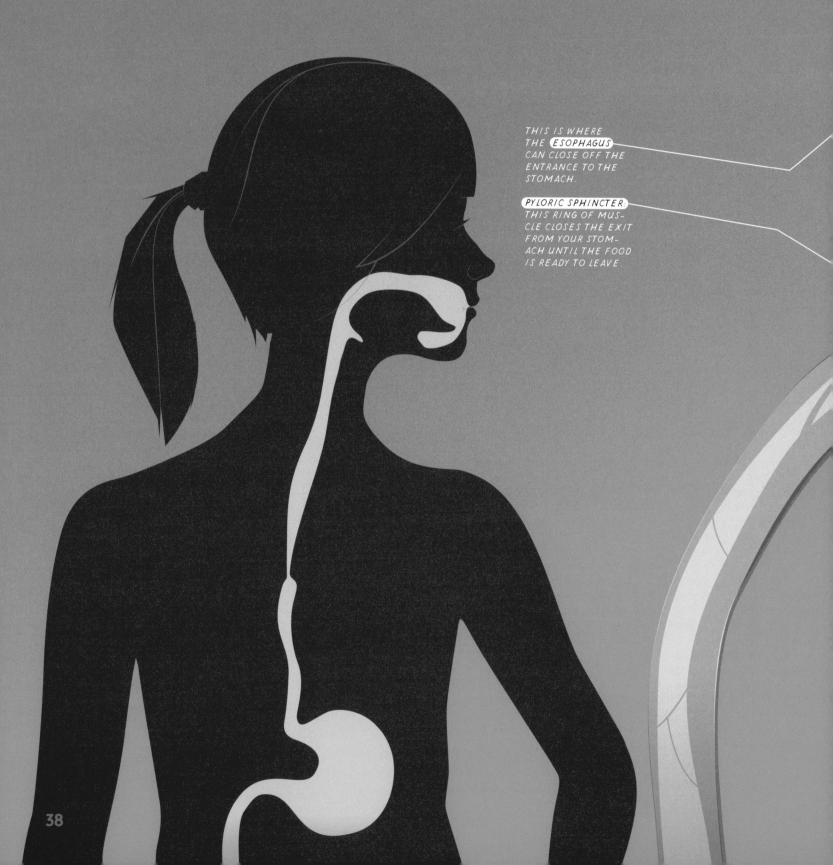

THIS IS WHERE THE (ESOPHAGUS) CAN CLOSE OFF THE ENTRANCE TO THE STOMACH.

PYLORIC SPHINCTER: THIS RING OF MUSCLE CLOSES THE EXIT FROM YOUR STOMACH UNTIL THE FOOD IS READY TO LEAVE.

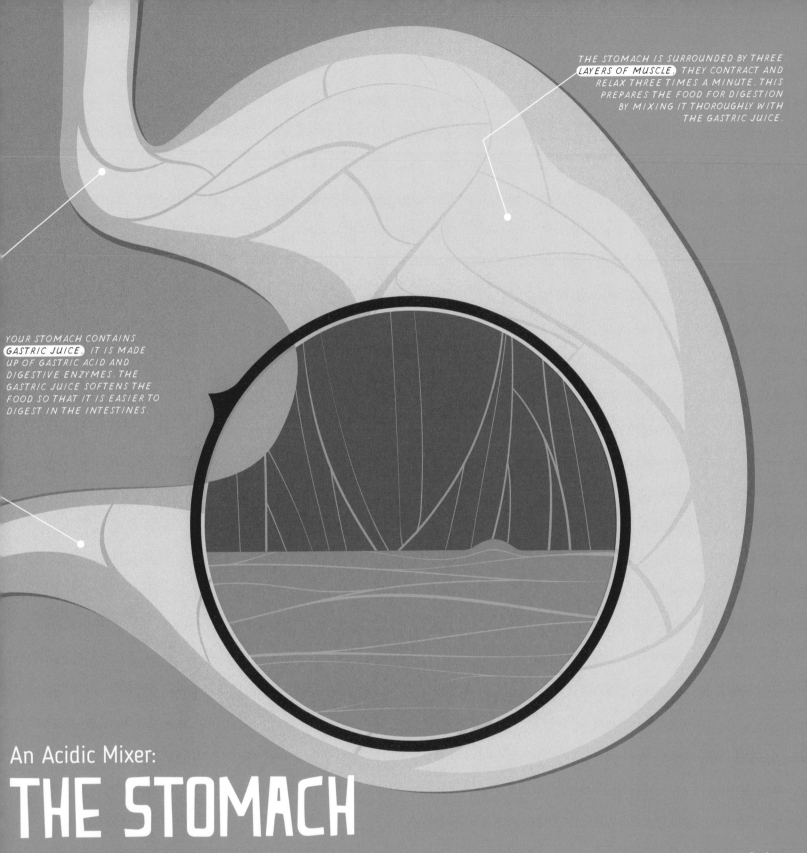

THE STOMACH IS SURROUNDED BY THREE LAYERS OF MUSCLE. THEY CONTRACT AND RELAX THREE TIMES A MINUTE. THIS PREPARES THE FOOD FOR DIGESTION BY MIXING IT THOROUGHLY WITH THE GASTRIC JUICE.

YOUR STOMACH CONTAINS GASTRIC JUICE. IT IS MADE UP OF GASTRIC ACID AND DIGESTIVE ENZYMES. THE GASTRIC JUICE SOFTENS THE FOOD SO THAT IT IS EASIER TO DIGEST IN THE INTESTINES.

An Acidic Mixer:

THE STOMACH

You've got hunger pangs and your belly's rumbling. One solution: a juicy burger and fries! But right after you've finished, you feel like you're full of cement. All you can think about is taking a nap so your stomach can do its work in peace. The muscles in your stomach contract three times a minute to churn the food up with your gastric juices. The juices work with enzymes to break down the burger and fries. Gastric acid is a nightmare for bacteria. It disinfects the food mush and starts to digest it. Our stomach is protected from the acid by an extra-thick layer of mucous that renews itself every three days. But even though hydrochloric acid is potent stuff, it can still take six hours to deal with fatty foods! Pretzels are easier. They leave the stomach after about two hours. The pyloric sphincter opens up and lets the mush pass into the intestines.

The Liver, Gallbladder, and Pancreas

If our stomach and intestines had to digest our food and drink all on their own, they'd probably go on strike. To do their job properly, they need help from three other organs: the liver, gallbladder, and pancreas. The liver is the biggest of the three. It works like a chemical plant by producing bile, a yellowish-green liquid that aids digestion and is stored in the gallbladder. Whenever we eat something fatty, our gallbladder contracts and sends bile into the duodenum. The pancreas also produces enzymes to help the digestion process. Other important liver functions include extracting the nutrients that entered the blood during digestion. This is how our food becomes energy and builds up our body. The liver also breaks down poisons like alcohol. The pancreas also has a non-digestive role. It keeps the blood topped up with exactly the right amount of insulin so that every cell in the body can absorb energy.

AN ADULT'S INTESTINES ARE ABOUT 16 FEET LONG. YOURS ARE PROBABLY A BIT SHORTER—BUT THEY WOULD STILL BE ABOUT AS TALL AS A GIRAFFE IF YOU UNRAVELED THEM!

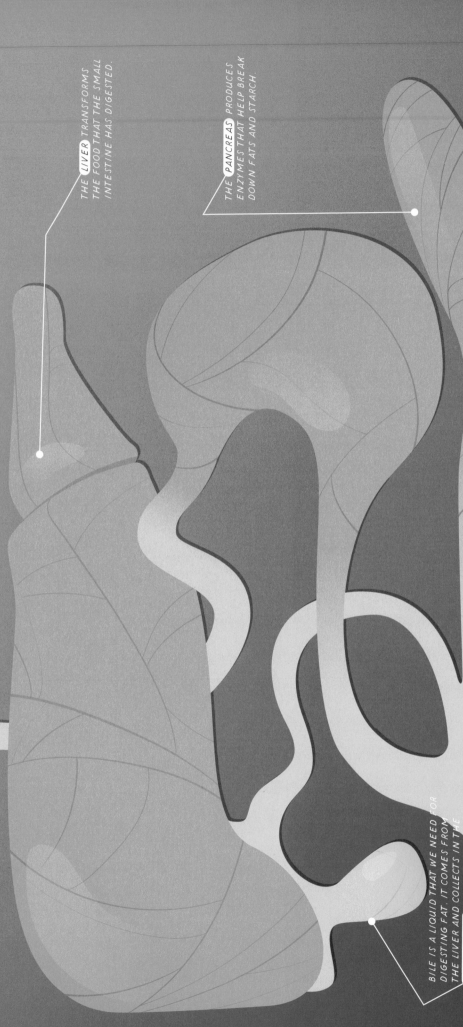

THE LIVER TRANSFORMS THE FOOD THAT THE SMALL INTESTINE HAS DIGESTED.

THE PANCREAS PRODUCES ENZYMES THAT HELP BREAK DOWN FATS AND STARCH.

BILE IS A LIQUID THAT WE NEED FOR DIGESTING FAT. IT COMES FROM THE LIVER AND COLLECTS IN THE GALLBLADDER.

THE SMALL INTESTINE FILTERS NUTRIENTS OUT OF THE FOOD AND PASSES THEM ON TO THE BLOOD, WHICH THEN FLOWS THROUGH THE LIVER.

THE LARGE INTESTINE REMOVES LIQUID FROM THE DIGESTED FOOD.

THE APPENDIX LIES IN BETWEEN THE SMALL AND LARGE INTESTINE. IT CAN SOMETIMES BECOME INFLAMED, WHICH IS REALLY PAINFUL.

Food Processers and Fart Factories:
THE INTESTINES

Any idea how often you fart? Most people toot about 14 times per day. Farts are caused by the bacteria (about 100 types) in our large intestine. They produce gas when they feed on undigested food waste. By the time your lunch reaches the large intestine, it's been processed by the small intestine and isn't really food anymore. The wall of the small intestine is covered in millions of hair-like protrusions called villi, which guide nutrients like fat, sugar, and protein into the blood. The large intestine turns the mush into a sausage shape by removing water from it. Next stop is the bathroom. But although the large intestine's bacteria are friendly, you still need to wash your hands!

41

Two Cleaners, One Water Bag:

THE KIDNEYS AND BLADDER

The kidneys are two bean-shaped organs about the size of a fist. They sit just below the bottom of our ribcage. Kidneys are vital, but it is possible to live with just one. Their job is to clean our blood—and they never, ever take a break. They clean about 3,000 pints of it every day. Of course, we don't have that much blood in our body. Adults only have about 10 pints, but it travels through the kidneys about 300 times per day. The kidneys clean the blood by removing substances that cannot stay in the body. These are dissolved in water and travel into the urinary bladder, which can swell to the size of a large grapefruit. At that point, the urine has to exit via the urethra. If you haven't drunk much, your urine will be darker because it contains less water. Interesting fact: urine has a very good reputation in some countries, where some people even drink it to quench their thirst. Also, a lot of creams on sale in our stores contain urea because it keeps the skin smooth and supple!

RIGHT KIDNEY

2 THE RENAL CORPUSCLES FILTER TOXINS AND WATER OUT OF THE BLOOD.

4 URINE COLLECTS IN THE BLADDER UNTIL IT IS READY TO BE EXPELLED.

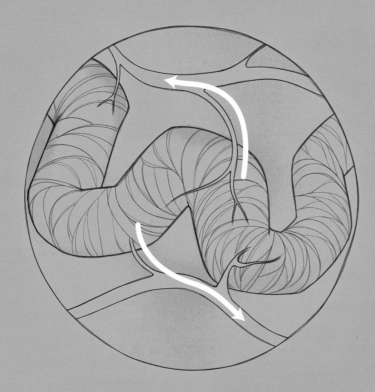

WHEN WE DRINK WATER, IT GETS INTO OUR BLOOD THROUGH THE INTESTINES. THE KIDNEYS HELP US GET RID OF EXCESS WATER AND OTHER SUBSTANCES.

42

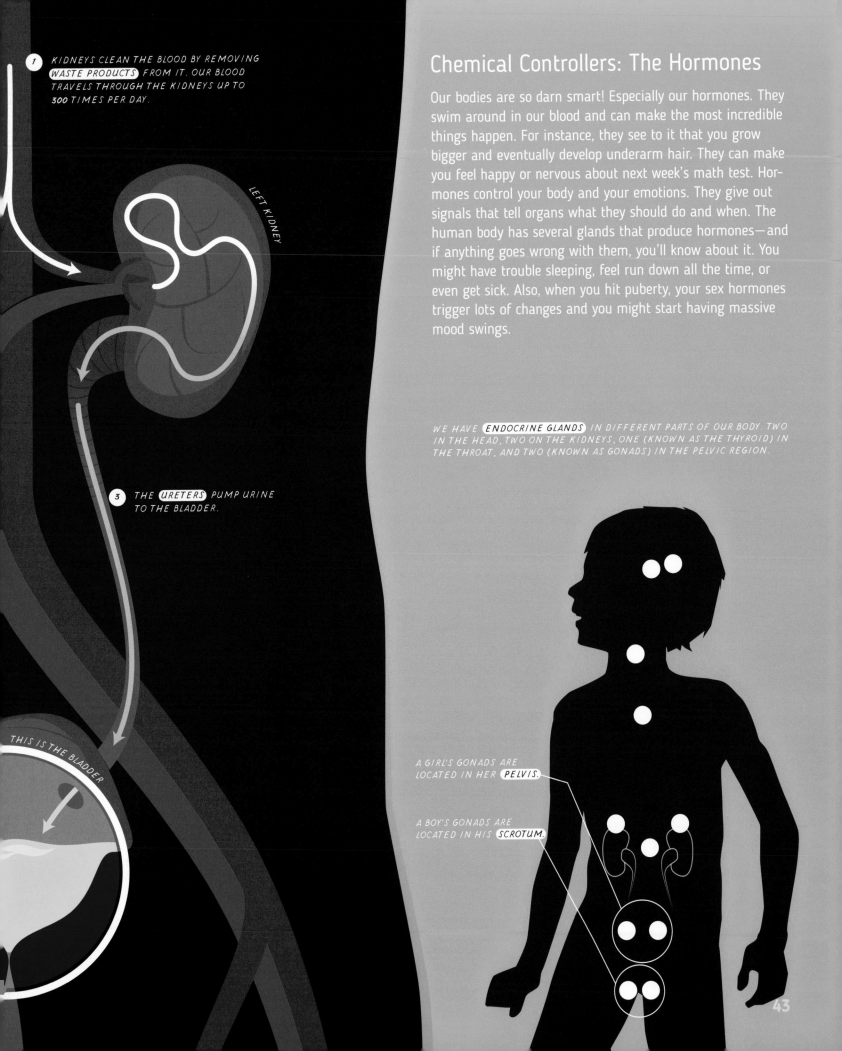

1 KIDNEYS CLEAN THE BLOOD BY REMOVING *WASTE PRODUCTS* FROM IT. OUR BLOOD TRAVELS THROUGH THE KIDNEYS UP TO *300* TIMES PER DAY.

LEFT KIDNEY

3 THE *URETERS* PUMP URINE TO THE BLADDER.

THIS IS THE BLADDER

Chemical Controllers: The Hormones

Our bodies are so darn smart! Especially our hormones. They swim around in our blood and can make the most incredible things happen. For instance, they see to it that you grow bigger and eventually develop underarm hair. They can make you feel happy or nervous about next week's math test. Hormones control your body and your emotions. They give out signals that tell organs what they should do and when. The human body has several glands that produce hormones—and if anything goes wrong with them, you'll know about it. You might have trouble sleeping, feel run down all the time, or even get sick. Also, when you hit puberty, your sex hormones trigger lots of changes and you might start having massive mood swings.

WE HAVE *ENDOCRINE GLANDS* IN DIFFERENT PARTS OF OUR BODY. TWO IN THE HEAD, TWO ON THE KIDNEYS, ONE (KNOWN AS THE THYROID) IN THE THROAT, AND TWO (KNOWN AS GONADS) IN THE PELVIC REGION.

A GIRL'S GONADS ARE LOCATED IN HER *PELVIS.*

A BOY'S GONADS ARE LOCATED IN HIS *SCROTUM.*

43

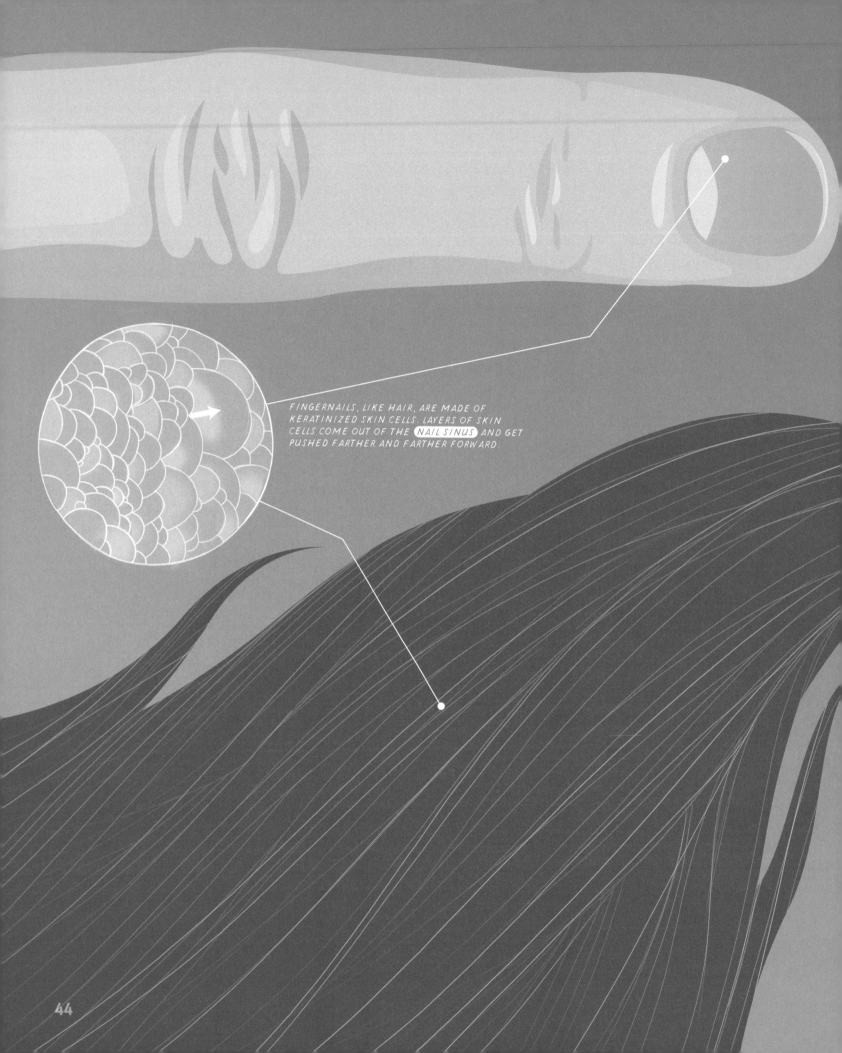

FINGERNAILS, LIKE HAIR, ARE MADE OF
KERATINIZED SKIN CELLS. LAYERS OF SKIN
CELLS COME OUT OF THE NAIL SINUS AND GET
PUSHED FARTHER AND FARTHER FORWARD.

Decoration and Protection:
THE HAIR AND NAILS

Hair and nails are made of keratinized skin cells. Although you don't feel anything when you cut your hair and nails, the roots of both are very much alive. They sit below the surface of the skin and are connected to muscles and neurons. Goosebumps happen when tiny muscles make the hairs on our skin stand on end. Also, here's a surprising hair fact: humans have as much hair as monkeys do! Most of ours is just much finer, shorter, and softer. Animals mainly need their fur to stop them from freezing. Clothes do the same job for us.

Our genes and hormones decide how much hair we have on different parts of our body and how thick it is. Some people have a lot of hair, while others have very little. The hair on our head grows about 0.08 inches per week, so just under half an inch per month. Individual hairs can stay connected to our head for several years. But even really long hair that might have been growing for two or three years will eventually fall out. When that happens, a new hair starts growing out of the same root. The type of hair a person has (straight, frizzy, or curly) depends on things called follicles. These sit just above the root out of which the hair grows. Round follicles produce straight hair, oval ones produce curly, and flat ones produce frizzy. Our nails also grow in different shapes—and they grow faster on the hand with which you write!

The Genes Decide:
Dark Hair or Blonde?

Even if both your parents have dark hair and yours is blonde, you still inherited your hair color from them. Where else could it have come from? This is how it works: both parents have one gene for dark hair and one gene for blonde hair. The reason they have dark hair is because the dark-hair gene is dominant and overrides the blonde-hair gene, which is recessive. Another thing that you inherit is the ability to roll your tongue—or not. This is a dominant trait, which means you just need to inherit one tongue-rolling gene to be able to do it. If you don't get the gene, you'll never be a tongue roller, no matter how hard you try.

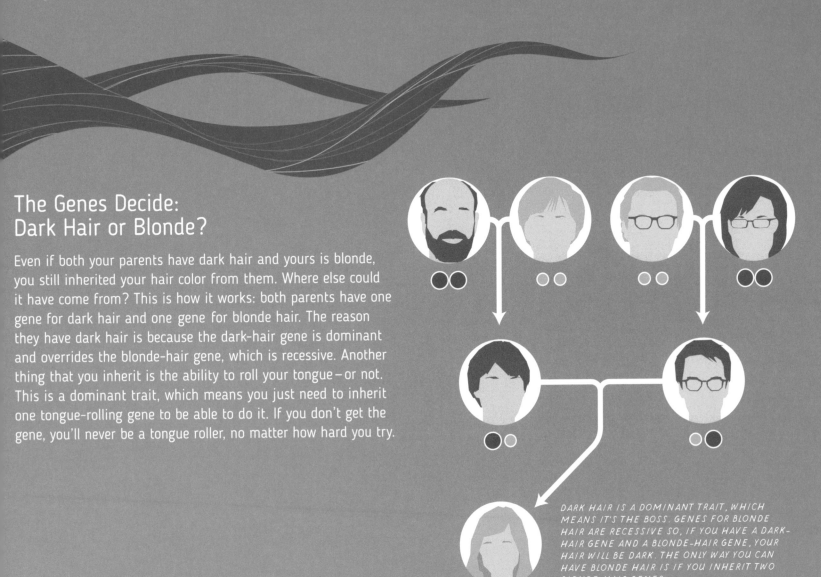

DARK HAIR IS A DOMINANT TRAIT, WHICH MEANS IT'S THE BOSS. GENES FOR BLONDE HAIR ARE RECESSIVE SO, IF YOU HAVE A DARK-HAIR GENE AND A BLONDE-HAIR GENE, YOUR HAIR WILL BE DARK. THE ONLY WAY YOU CAN HAVE BLONDE HAIR IS IF YOU INHERIT TWO BLONDE-HAIR GENES.

Teamwork:
REPRODUCTION

If we were like ringed worms, we'd be able to reproduce all on our own. These little critters just break off a part of themselves and, hey presto, it turns into a brand new worm! But we humans have to reproduce in pairs. Reproduction happens when a man's sperm fuses with a woman's egg. To make sure our species doesn't die out, nature has made sure that (sex) feels really nice and that people (once they're old enough) enjoy having it. When a man and a woman have sex, the man ejaculates and releases sperm into the woman's vagina. The sperm then swim towards the woman's egg and try to fertilize it. Even though there are millions of sperm, only one of them can penetrate the egg. If everything goes according to plan, the fertilized egg travels along the fallopian tube and into the woman's uterus, where it settles. After that, the cells begin to divide and develop into arms, legs, eyes, and everything else a person needs to live. Nine months later, the process comes to an end and a little baby is born.

Boys' Stuff: Penis and Testicles

Big, small, long, fat, straight, or curved: every boy's penis looks a bit different. That's even truer for men, as the differences are more noticeable once the penis has reached its full size. But it doesn't matter what a penis looks like because every penis can its job just fine. In fact, a penis has two jobs: it is the tube that takes urine out of the body, and it helps make babies later on in life. When a boy reaches puberty—usually sometime between ages 11 and 15—his body starts changing so that he can grow into a man. His penis and testicles will get bigger and pubic hair will appear. Also, he'll start to have sexual feelings that make his penis hard. The feelings send lots of blood flowing into the erectile tissue in his penis, which causes it to stand up. This can happen to younger children, too. Sometime during puberty, boys will ejaculate for the first time. It often happens at night, which is completely normal and nothing to worry about. Ejaculation is when millions of (sperm) leave the testicles and come out of the penis. The reason there are so many sperm is that only one of them can fertilize an egg, so nature is increasing their chances of success. This only becomes important later, when the boy has grown up and wants to make a baby. One more thing: it's always the man's sperm that determines if a fertilized egg grows into a baby girl or a baby boy.

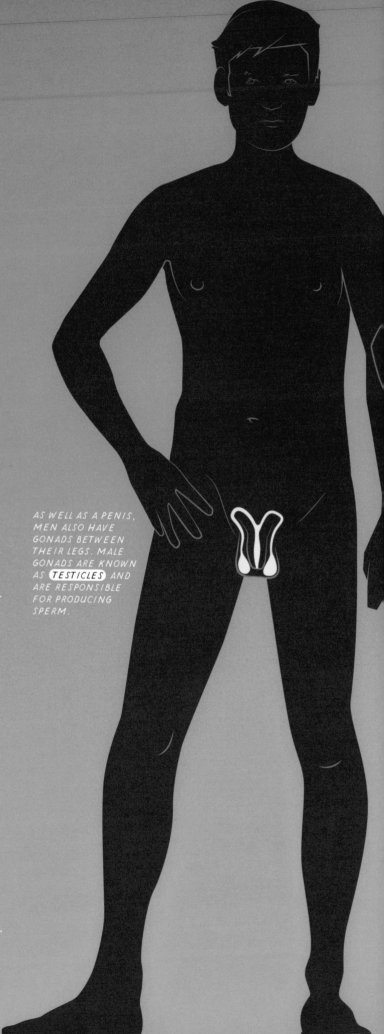

AS WELL AS A PENIS, MEN ALSO HAVE GONADS BETWEEN THEIR LEGS. MALE GONADS ARE KNOWN AS TESTICLES AND ARE RESPONSIBLE FOR PRODUCING SPERM.

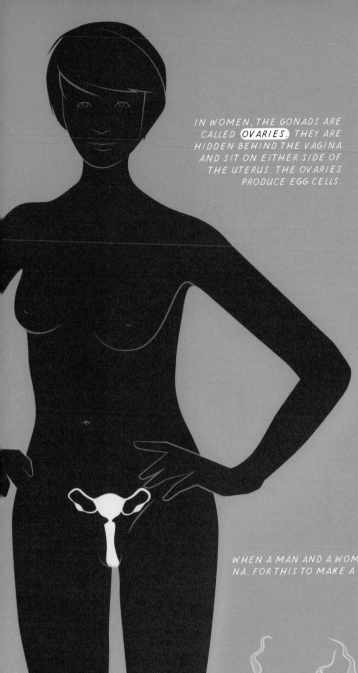

Girls' Stuff: Vulva, Vagina, Ovaries, and Uterus

IN WOMEN, THE GONADS ARE CALLED OVARIES. THEY ARE HIDDEN BEHIND THE VAGINA AND SIT ON EITHER SIDE OF THE UTERUS. THE OVARIES PRODUCE EGG CELLS.

While the word "vagina" is widely used to refer to the female sexual organ, "vulva" would be more accurate, but it's not so popular. The vulva refers to a number of different organs: the clitoris, the labia, and the opening to the vagina. The vagina is a tube that leads from the vulva to the cervix. When girls hit puberty, lots of things start changing, including their vulva, which will get bigger and grow pubic hair. No two vulvas ever look the same. Sometime between ages 10 and 14, girls will get their first period. Once that happens, the sex hormones are in charge. The ovaries (which are in the abdomen) will release an egg once a month, and the uterus will expel blood every month if that egg is not fertilized. By the way, urine doesn't come out of the vagina—it comes out of the urethra, which exits just above the vaginal opening.

WHEN A MAN AND A WOMAN HAVE SEX, THE MAN EJACULATES, WHICH RELEASES SPERM INTO THE WOMAN'S VAGINA. FOR THIS TO MAKE A BABY, THE FOLLOWING THINGS HAVE TO OCCUR:

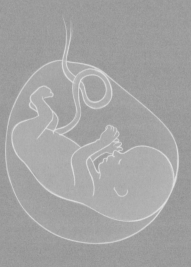

1 *MILLIONS OF SPERM SWIM TO-WARDS THE EGG—BUT ONLY ONE SPERM CAN PENETRATE THE EGG AND FERTILIZE IT.*

2 *THE SPERM AND THE EGG FUSE TO FORM ONE CELL. THE CELL STARTS DIVIDING AND GRADUALLY MULTIPLIES. THIS FORMS AN EMBRYO THAT GROWS INTO A FOETUS.*

3 *AFTER NINE MONTHS IN THE UTERUS, WHERE IT RECEIVES ALL THE NUTRIENTS IT NEEDS, THE BABY IS READY TO LEAVE ITS MOTHER'S BODY AND ENTER THE WORLD AS A NEWBORN.*

MY BODY

EXPLAINED AND ILLUSTRATED

This book was conceived and edited by Little Gestalten.

Texts by Antje Helms
Illustrations, layout, and captions by Golden Section Graphics

Fact-checking by Cord-Hinnerk Delventhal
Translation from German by Jen Metcalf
Proofreading by Felix Lennert

Published by Little Gestalten, an imprint of Die Gestalten Verlag GmbH & Co. KG, Berlin 2015
ISBN: 978-3-89955-712-1

A German edition titled *Mein Körper* is available under the ISBN 978-3-89955-711-4.

Typefaces: Blogger Sans by Sergiy Tkachenko; Peach Milk by Frédéric Rich; Tintin

Printed by Offsetdruckerei Grammlich, Pliezhausen
Made in Germany

For more information, please visit little.gestalten.com.

Bibliographic information published by the Deutsche Nationalbibliothek:
The Deutsche Nationalbibliothek lists this publication in the Deutsche Nationalbibliografie; detailed bibliographic data are available online at http://dnb.d-nb.de.

This book was printed on paper certified according to the standards of the FSC®.